Pearson

Pearson Edexcel GCSE

Spanish

Vocabulary, Grammar and Translation Workbook

Denise Currie and Leanda Reeves

Published by Pearson Education Limited, 80 Strand, London, WC2R ORL.

www.pearsonschoolsandfecolleges.co.uk

Copies of official specifications for all Pearson qualifications may be found on the website: qualifications.pearson.com

Edited by Newgen KnowledgeWorks

Designed and typeset by Kamae Design and Newgen KnowledgeWorks

Original illustrations © Pearson Education Limited 2025

Illustrated by Beehive Illustrations: Andrew Pagram, Alan Rowe and Matt Ward. Further illustrations created by Johanna Crainmark and Newgen KnowledgeWorks

Cover design by Kamae Design

Cover photo and banner extract © Pierre Maheux/Getty Images

Written by Denise Currie and Leanda Reeves

Select content created using AI based on Pearson learning materials. To maintain the integrity of content in this product, Pearson has a process to validate output prior to publication.

Printed in the UK by Bell & Bain Ltd, Glasgow

First published 2025

29 28 27 26 25

10 9 8 7 6 5 4 3 2 1

British Library Cataloguing in Publication Data
A catalogue record for this book is available from the British Library

ISBN 978 1 292 489582

Notes from the publisher
Pearson has robust editorial processes, including answer and fact checks, to ensure the accuracy of the content in this publication, and every effort is made to ensure this publication is free of errors. We are, however, only human, and occasionally errors do occur. Pearson is not liable for any misunderstandings that arise as a result of errors in this publication, but it is our priority to ensure that the content is accurate. If you spot an error, please do contact us at resourcescorrections@pearson.com so we can make sure it is corrected.

Contenidos

Basic language

1 Complete the sentences with a suitable word(s) from the box. There are more words than gaps.

adiós gracias hola momento perdón por favor provecho segundo señora vale

1. ¡...Hola.......Alba! Buenas tardes. ¿Qué tal estás?
2. Quisiera un café, ...
3. Buenos días, ..señora... ¿Va al restaurante? ¡Buen ...provecho
4. Vamos en autobús, ¿..Vale.........?
5. Buenas noches, señor....perdón no tengo tiempo, pero ...gracias por su ayuda.
6. ....~~Vale~~..., mamá. Voy a Medellín. Hasta luego. Adiós

2 Give the correct number in figures.

1. mil ...1000...
2. quince ...15...
3. trece ...13...
4. veintiuno ...21...
5. un millón ...1000000...
6. catorce ...14...
7. cien ...100...

> **G** **Cardinal** numbers are numbers that show quantity (such as *uno, dos, tres...*).
> **Ordinal** numbers allow you to express order (such as *primero, segundo, tercero...*).

3 Continue the sequence in words.

1. siete, ocho, nueve, diez, once, ~~se~~ doce...
2. dieciséis, diecisiete, dieciocho, diecinueve, ..viente.....
3. treinta, cuarenta, cincuenta, sesenta, setenta, ochenta, ..noventa
4. cero, uno, dos, tres, cuatro, cinco, ...sies.......
5. primero, segundo, tercero, cuarto, ...cinto... quinto

4 Solve the puzzle by completing the sentences with the correct day, month or season in Spanish.

1. Junio, julio y ...agosto. son los meses de verano.
2. Diciembre, enero y febrero son los meses de ..invierno..
3. Me gusta salir los .sabados. y domingos.
4. El día después del miércoles es ....~~viernes~~ jueves
5. Mi día favorito es el día antes del martes. Es el ..lunes.....
6. Prefiero la primavera: los meses de marzo, abril y ..mayo.......
7. En el colegio prefiero el ..vienes... porque es el día antes del fin de semana.
8. Los meses de septiembre, octubre y .noviembre son los meses de otoño.

> In Spanish, days of the week, months of the year and seasons do not have capital letters.

> These colour words agree in gender and number: *negro, blanco, rojo, amarillo.*
> These colour words agree in number: *azul, verde, gris, marrón.*
> These colour words are invariable (do not change): *rosa, naranja.*

5 Write the correct letter to match up the sentence halves.

1 Mañana por la tarde Omar		a	fuiste al colegio al mediodía.
2 Ayer a las once y media yo	lK	b	están muy lejos.
3 Hoy mi hermano se levanta	Ko	c	son ciudades españolas.
4 Ayer tú	a	d	son países de América Latina.
5 Las clases duran	i	e	se celebra en Latinoamérica.
6 Esta noche a las nueve tú	m	f	el primer año del siglo.
7 El Día de los Muertos	e	g	son islas españolas.
8 Las Fallas de Valencia	n	h	va a ir a las Islas Canarias.
9 La Tomatina	p	i	una hora y diez minutos.
10 Barcelona y Madrid	c	j	está dentro de Europa.
11 Venezuela y Bolivia	d	k	me levanto muy temprano.
12 Las Islas Baleares	g	l	comí algo.
13 El Reino Unido	j	m	vas a salir.
14 Asia y África		n	se celebran en España.
H 15 El año 2000 fue	f	o	por la mañana.
H 16 Al principio del día		p	es una fiesta española.

H 6 Complete the sentences with the correct form of the adjective in brackets.

1 El traje de mi padre es azul (*azul*)
2 Mis zapatos son marrónes (*marrón*)
3 La señora tiene unos pañuelos rojos (*rojo*)
4 El paisaje aquí es muy verde (*verde*)
5 Mi jersey preferido es rosa (*rosa*)
6 Debes ponerte los calcetines narangjas (*naranja*)
7 A Papá le gusta llevar las zapatillas de deporte blancos (*blanco*)
8 Sofía compró unos auriculares negros (*negro*)

F 7 Translate these sentences into Spanish.

1 My favourite colour is yellow. Mi color gavorita es amarillo
2 I do not like the end of December. No me gusta el sin de Deciembro
3 I celebrated New Year's Eve with my family. Celebré el sin de año con mi gamilia
4 My father goes to Buenos Aires for Carnival. Mi padre va a Buenos Aires para el Carnival
5 At the beginning of the year, I am happy. Al inicio del año, estoy geliz

H 8 Translate this paragraph into English on a separate sheet.

Cada semana voy a casa de mis abuelos. Durante la primera parte del día paso tiempo en el jardín. La última vez vi unos pájaros allí. Suelo ir el sábado por la tarde cuando hay menos tráfico. Mi abuela es de Ecuador en América Latina, pero vive aquí en Barcelona desde el principio de su carrera.

Zona de cultura El mundo hispanohablante

Using adjectives in Spanish

1 Draw lines to match up the sentence halves. Then translate the sentences into English.

1 Me llamo Omar y soy
2 Es una persona
3 Mi amigo
4 Mi nombre es Fátima y
5 Mis amigas son

a es argentino.
b soy española.
c muy buena.
d colombianas.
e simpático.

Me llamo Omar y soy argentino
Es una persona muy buena
My griend is grom Argentina
My name is Fatima and I am
My griends are Colombian

2 Draw lines to match up the questions with the answers.

1 ¿Cómo te llamas?
2 ¿De dónde eres?
3 ¿Cómo eres?
4 ¿Dónde se habla español?

a Soy de Latinoamérica.
b Se habla español en veintiún países.
c Mi nombre es Teresa, pero yo prefiero Tere.
d Creo que soy muy tranquila.

G

Adjectives agree with the noun they describe.

masculine singular	feminine singular	masculine plural	feminine plural
mal**o** interesant**e** difícil trabajador	mal**a** interesant**e** difícil trabajador**a**	mal**os** interesant**es** difícil**es** trabajador**es**	mal**as** interesant**es** difícil**es** trabajador**as**

3 Circle the correct adjective to complete each sentence.

1 Soy una persona **simpático** / **simpática** / **simpáticos** / **simpáticas**.
2 El ciclismo es un deporte muy **divertido** / **divertida** / **divertidos** / **divertidas**.
3 Creo que el fútbol es **increíble** / **increíbles**.
H 4 Nació en Ecuador y mucha gente dice que es una persona **feliz** / **felices**.
H 5 Yo diría que mi amigo argentino es muy **práctico** / **práctica** / **prácticos** / **prácticas**.

4 Complete the table. Then complete the sentences about famous people.

cubano	cubana	cubanos	cubanas
chileano	chilena	chileanos	chileanas
colombiano	colombiana	colombianos	colombianas
español	española	españoles	españolas

1  Mi nombre ...es... Ana de Armas y soy ...Cubana... (*Cuba*).

2  Me ...llamo... Pedro Pascal y soy ...Chileano... (*Chile*).

3  Su nombre ...es... Ángel Barajas y es ...Colombiana?... (*Colombia*).

Spanish 4  Se ...llama... Vicky López y es ...Española... (*Spain*).

> **G**
> Adjectives in Spanish generally follow the noun they describe.
> *El chico* ***español*** *es una persona* ***segura****.*
> Some adjectives can come before the noun but they change their spelling.
> *primero* → *primer* *Aprendemos los países en español el* ***primer*** *día de clase.*
> *bueno* → *buen* *Es un* ***buen*** *amigo.*

5 Underline the adjectives. Then unjumble the words to rewrite the sentences correctly.

1 Karima soy llamo persona y Me una interesante ...Me llamo Karima y soy una persona interesante...

2 que una Creo soy persona social ...Creo que soy una persona social...

H 3 dicen soy persona optimista que amigos una Mis ...Mis amigos dicen que soy una persona optimista...

H 4 que Pienso madre muy práctica mi soy como ...Pienso que soy muy práctica como mi madre...

F 6 Translate these sentences into English.

1 Soy trabajador como mi madre. ...I am hardworking like my mum....

2 El español es una lengua popular. ...Spanish is a popular language....

3 Creo que el deporte es increíble. ...I think sport is incredible....

4 Todos mis amigos son españoles. ...All my friends are Spanish....

His or her? (his) Remember that *no* can be translated as 'no' or 'not'.

5 Su nombre es Pablo y creo que no es una buena persona. ...His name is Pablo and I don't think he's a good person....

H 7 Translate this paragraph into Spanish.

I am Nadia and I am Peruvian. I think that I am quite social. My friend Vicente thinks that I am a calm person. He was born on the eighth of April and he is from Venezuela. In Venezuela more than thirty-three million people speak Spanish. It's an incredible country.

Soy Nadia y soy Peruviana. (Peruana) Pienso que soy bastante social. Mi amigo Vicente piensa que soy una persona calma. (tranquila) Nació en el octavo (ocho) de Abril y es de Venezuela. En Venezuela, más de trencha y tres mil (millones de) personas hablan Español. Es un país increíble.

1 Decide whether these words are nouns (N), verbs (V) or adverbs of frequency (AF). Then translate the words into English.

chateo	siempre	prefiero ....
haces	usamos	**usuarios** ....
a veces	leo	**grabamos** ....
escuchamos	música	**pantalla** ....
imagenes	ordenador	**documentales** ....
nunca	a menudo	**utilizan** ....
subo	móvil	**aparato** ....

2 Complete the missing verbs in parallel sentences. Use verbs from the box in exercise 1.

1	We often use apps.	A menudo .... aplicaciones.
2	I sometimes .... photos.	A veces subo fotos.
3	I never read the news.	Nunca .... las noticias.
4	Do you .... purchases online?	¿Haces compras en línea?
5	I prefer to search for information on my phone.	.... buscar información en mi móvil.
H 6	She almost never records videos.	Casi nunca .... vídeos.
H 7	.... a lot of equipment.	Utilizan muchos aparatos.

G

Remember to form the **present tense** by removing **-ar**, **-er** or **-ir** from the infinitive and adding the following endings.

	tom**ar** (*to take*)	le**er** (*to read*)	viv**ir** (*to live*)
(yo)	tom**o**	le**o**	viv**o**
(tú)	tom**as**	le**es**	viv**es**
(él/ella/usted)	tom**a**	le**e**	viv**e**
(nosotros/as)	tom**amos**	le**emos**	viv**imos**
(vosotros/as)	tom**áis**	le**éis**	viv**ís**
(ellos/ellas/ustedes)	tom**an**	le**en**	viv**en**

3 Complete the endings of the regular *-ar*, *-er* and *-ir* verbs below.

mand**ar** – to send	cre**er** – to believe/think	recib**ir** – to receive
mand........	cre........	recib........
mand........	cre........	recib........
mand........	cre........	recib........
mand........	cre........	recib........
mand........	cre........	recib........
mand........	cre........	recib........

4 Circle the correct verb to complete each sentence.

1 Yo siempre **pasas** / **paso** / **pasamos** tres horas al día con la videoconsola porque me encantan los juegos.

2 Mohammed **lees** / **lee** / **leen** las noticias porque piensa que es necesario.

3 ¿Qué **hago** / **hacen** / **haces** en tu ordenador normalmente?

4 Mis amigos y yo **preferimos** / **prefiero** / **prefieren** las aplicaciones como Instagram para recibir mensajes.

H 5 Carolina **utilizamos** / **utilizo** / **utiliza** un aparato electrónico para mantenerse en contacto con su familia.

H 6 Mis padres no **usan** / **usas** / **usáis** auriculares cuando se conectan a Internet.

G

Some verbs are **stem-changing**.

u/o → ue		e → ie		
j**u**gar → j**ue**go	p**o**der → p**ue**do	pref**e**rir → prefi**e**ro	qu**e**rer → qui**e**ro	p**e**nsar → pi**e**nso
j**ue**gas	p**ue**des	prefi**e**res	qui**e**res	pi**e**nsas
j**ue**ga	p**ue**de	prefi**e**re	qui**e**re	pi**e**nsa
jugamos	podemos	preferimos	queremos	pensamos
jugáis	podéis	preferís	queréis	pensáis
j**ue**gan	p**ue**den	prefi**e**ren	qui**e**ren	pi**e**nsan

H 5 Complete the sentences by conjugating the infinitive correctly.

1 Los usuarios de la web .... (*preferir*) las aplicaciones con contraseñas.

2 Mis amigas y yo .... (*jugar*) a un juego en línea los domingos.

3 Y vosotras, ¿cuántas horas .... (*querer*) pasar al día con vuestros aparatos?

4 Yo siempre .... (*utilizar*) la pantalla de mi móvil para ver vídeos deportivos.

5 Los jóvenes .... (*poder*) colgar muchas fotos divertidas.

F 6 Translate these sentences into Spanish.

1 I often listen to music. ....

2 My friend does not send emails. ....

3 She always uploads funny photos every night. ....

4 Sometimes we send private messages online. ....

5 Young people spend a lot of time on social media. ....

H 7 Translate this paragraph into English on a separate sheet.

Veo documentales o grabo vídeos con mis amigos. De vez en cuando jugamos con algún aparato de realidad virtual. Una de mis amigas cree que las redes sociales son fáciles para mandar y recibir mensajes. Muchos jóvenes no utilizan contraseñas en todas las aplicaciones de sus ordenadores portátiles. Mis padres piensan que tener muchos seguidores desconocidos es peligroso.

Remember that infinitives can be translated with '-ing'.

2 ¡Disfrutamos al máximo!

Revising irregular present tense verbs

1 Draw lines to match up the sentence halves.

1 Odio el
2 Me encantan
3 Creo que la
4 Si tenemos dinero, nos gusta
H 5 Si tengo tiempo, voy

a los libros de ciencia ficción porque me interesan mucho.
b al gimnasio para mantenerme en contacto con mis amigos.
c vóleibol porque creo que es difícil y aburrido.
d ir al cine para ver películas de aventura.
e natación es un deporte guay.

2 Read each sentence. Tick ✓ if they are true for you or correct them to make them true.

1 ~~Me~~ gusta el fútbol porque es ~~emocionante~~. ✗

No me gusta el fútbol porque es aburrido.

2 Soy miembro de un club de música porque es emocionante. ✗

No soy miembro de un clube de musica porque es difícil

3 Mi pasatiempo favorito es ver series porque es relajante. ✓

4 Soy aficionado/a a montar a caballo porque es mi pasión. ✗

No me gusta montar a

5 En mi opinión, el baile es una actividad fácil. ✗

En mi opinión, el baile

H 6 Me encanta ver comedias o musicales en el cine. ✓

H 7 Para estar en forma siempre practico atletismo. ✗

Para estar en sorma voy al parque con mi madre.

G

Ir, ***ser*** and ***tener*** are important irregular verbs in the present tense.

	ir (*to go*)	**ser** (*to be*)	**tener** (*to have*)
(yo)	voy	soy	tengo
(tú)	vas	eres	tienes
(él/ella/usted)	va	es	tiene
(nosotros/as)	vamos	somos	tenemos
(vosotros/as)	vais	sois	tenéis
(ellos/ellas/ustedes)	van	son	tienen

However, some verbs are only irregular in the first person (I):

hacer → ***hago*** (I do/make)
salir → ***salgo*** (I go out)
ver → ***veo*** (I see)
dar → ***doy*** (I give)
saber → ***sé*** (I know)

3 Complete the table with the correct verb.

subject	hacer	ir	ser	tener	ver
Yo	hago	voy	soy	tengo	vejo
Omar y yo	hacemos	vamos	somos	tenemos	vemos
Mi amigo	hace	vay	es	tiene	ve
Mis amigos	hacen	van	son	tienen	veen

4 Circle the correct verb and write the correct nouns in Spanish.

1 Me **gustan** / **gusta** mucho el fútbol porque es mi pasión. (*football*)

2 Mis amigos y yo **son** / **somos** aficionados al baloncesto. (*basketball*)

3 Yo siempre **leo** / **lee** muchos libros y revistas porque es divertido. (*books*)

4 Nos **encanta** / **encantan** ver las pelicolas de terror nuevas. (*films*)

H 5 Si **tiene** / **tienen** tiempo, mis amigos escuchan musica clásica y bailan. (*music*)

H 6 Os gusta hacer deportes como la natacion y **son** / **sois** miembros de un club. (*swimming*)

H 5 Rewrite the text below, so that it is in the third person singular (he/she) form.

Tengo varios pasatiempos divertidos que me gusta hacer. Si tengo dinero, siempre voy al cine para ver películas de comedia o de terror. Mi deporte favorito es el fútbol y creo que soy un jugador bastante bueno. Juego en un equipo profesional del Reino Unido y siempre me encanta el ambiente durante los partidos.

As well as verbs, remember to look out for pronouns that may need changing (e.g. **mi**).

Tiene varios pasatiempos divertidos que ~~me~~ le gusta hacer. Si tiene dinero, siempre vaj al cine para ver películas de comedia o de terror. Su deporte favorito es el fútobol y crea que es un jugador bastante bueno. Juega en en equipo profesional del Reino Unido y siempre le encanta el ambiente durante los partidos.

F 6 Translate these sentences into English.

1 Me encanta bailar en mi tiempo libre. I love to dance in my free time

2 Nunca vamos a la piscina. We never go to the pool

Think about order of adjectives and nouns.

3 También escucho muchas canciones relajantes. I also listen to relaxing songs

4 Los viernes monto a caballo y mi hermana lee revistas. On Tuesday I go horseriding and my sister reads magazines.

5 Si tenemos dinero, preferimos ir al estadio para ver un partido. If we have money, we prefer to go to the stadium to see a match

Use the infinitive.

H 7 Translate this paragraph into Spanish on a separate sheet.

Normally on Saturdays we play basketball. It's a fun sport. For me, doing hobbies helps me to stay in contact with my friends. My friend reads a lot but I am a fan of films and series. I also prefer to listen to lots of songs on my phone with my headphones.

How will *mucho* change its ending?

3 Nos juntamos

Using the near future

1 Draw lines to match up the questions with the answers. Then translate each question into English.

1 ¿Cómo estás?
2 ¿Tienes planes el jueves?
3 ¿Quieres venir conmigo a un concierto?
4 ¿A qué hora quedamos?
5 ¿Qué tienes que hacer?
6 ¿Qué películas ponen?

a Quedamos a las cuatro y cuarto.
b No, no tengo planes.
c Claro que sí. Me encanta el cantante.
d Esta tarde ponen dos películas de ciencia ficción.
e Tengo que ir de compras.
f Estoy bastante bien. ¿Y tú?

How are you?
Do you have plans on Thursday?
Do you want to come with me to a concert
What time do we arrive?
What do you do?
What films ~~do you watch~~ are on?

2 Complete each phrase with an infinitive. Then write the English translations.

ir cuidar estar limpiar mandar salir

1 [ir] de compras go shopping
2 [mandar] mensajes a mi novia message my girlfriend
3 [estar] en casa stay at home
4 [limpar] mi habitación clean my house
5 [salir] con mis abuelos go out with my Grandparents
H 6 [cuidar] a mi perro take care of my dog

3 Use the verbs in the grammar box to translate these sentences.

1 We are going to relax.
Vamos a relajar
2 They are going to find something.
Van a encontrar algo
3 I am going to dance.
Voy bailar
4 She is going to play. ~~Va~~ Va a ~~brincar~~ jugar
5 He is going to drink. Va a beber
6 Are you going to go? Vas ir?
7 You are (all) going to listen. Van escuchar

G

Use the **near future tense** to say what you are going to do in the future. It is made up of three parts:
present tense of *ir* + *a* + infinitive

(yo)	voy		beber	ir
(tú)	vas		bailar	jugar
(él/ella/usted)	va	a	descansar	salir
(nosotros/as)	vamos		empezar	ser
(vosotros/as)	vais		encontrar	tener
(ellos/ellas/ustedes)	van		escuchar	

4 Circle the correct form of the verb *ir* to complete the verbs in the near future.

1 La próxima semana yo **voy** / **vas** / **va** a practicar deporte.

2 Este fin de semana la película **voy** / **vas** / **va** a ser muy buena.

3 Luego, mi novio y yo **van** / **vamos** / **vas** a ir al parque para escuchar a la banda.

4 El miembro del club de fútbol **vais** / **van** / **va** a jugar por la mañana.

H 5 La sesión **van** / **vais** / **va** a empezar a las siete y media.

H 6 Los lectores **van** / **va** / **vas** a disfrutar del libro nuevo.

G

Tener que, ***querer*** and ***poder*** can be used with infinitives to talk about future plans. Remember that ***querer*** and ***poder*** are both stem-changing verbs.

Tenemos que *ir al cine.*
We have to go to the cinema.
Quiero *hablar contigo.*
I want to talk to you.
Puedes *venir mañana.*
You can come tomorrow.

H 5 Unjumble the Spanish and complete the English sentences.

1 la ¿ el quieres por sábado hacer qué ? tarde ....

2 hacer quiero mis salir y primero deberes luego podemos ....

3 vas parque ? domingo al a ¿ ir el ....

4 que porque mi va y a tengo hacer hermano ir atletismo ....

5 hasta tenis el podemos ¡ jugar al en perfecto el parque a ¡ domingo vamos ....

a What do you .... to do on .... afternoon?

b First, I want to do my .... and then we can ....

c Are you going .... the park on ....

d .... to go because my brother is going to do ....

e Perfect. We can play .... in the .... Until Sunday

F 6 Translate these sentences into Spanish.

1 I have plans for today. ....

2 We meet at the shopping centre. ....

3 He/She has to go to the cinema. ....

4 I am sorry, but I have to go out. ....

5 Tomorrow morning we are going to go shopping. ....

H 7 Translate this paragraph into English on a separate sheet.

Me llamo Indra y me gustan los libros. A menudo tengo planes con mi amigo Jalil. Pasamos mucho tiempo en su casa, donde nos gusta leer novelas o escuchar música en la cadena de sonido. Nunca queremos hacer los deberes hasta el domingo. El próximo sábado va a descansar, entonces yo voy a ir de compras.

Cadena is usually a 'channel' or 'chain' and *sonido* is 'sound' but look at the context. What is a *cadena de sonido*?

4 El fin de semana pasado

Using the preterite tense

1 Draw lines to match up the sentence halves.

1 Fuimos	**a** al baloncesto en la calle.
2 Jugué	**b** mucho por Internet ayer.
3 Hablé	**c** una serie de Netflix en la tele.
4 Vimos	**d** a un concierto para ver a una banda.
5 Tomé	**e** nada en casa en todo el día.
6 Gané	**f** un café antes de salir.
7 No hicimos	**g** un partido de fútbol con mi equipo.

2 Complete these sentences with the correct verb. Translate each sentence into English.

1 Hace dos días (*I went*) .... a un restaurante bueno.

....

2 El mes pasado (*we bought*) .... cuatro entradas para el concierto.

....

3 No me gustó nada el programa porque (*it was*) .... terrible.

....

4 La chica (*listened to*) .... la canción, pero no le gustó el ritmo.

el ritmo	*rhythm*

....

H **5** ¿(*Did you win*) .... la copa ayer en la competición?

....

H **6** (*They went*) .... a la gira mundial de su cantante favorito de música pop.

....

G

Use the **preterite** for completed actions in the past.

cant**ar** (*to sing*)	beb**er** (*to drink*)	sal**ir** (*to go out*)
cant**é** cant**aste** cant**ó** cant**amos** cant**asteis** cant**aron**	beb**í** beb**iste** beb**ió** beb**imos** beb**isteis** beb**ieron**	sal**í** sal**iste** sal**ió** sal**imos** sal**isteis** sal**ieron**

3 Rewrite these sentences in the preterite tense and add a suitable past time reference (e.g. *ayer*).

1 Escucho música *rock* en casa. Ayer escuché música *rock* en casa.

2 Bebemos mucho café en la cafetería. ....

3 Disfruto de una tarde divertida con mis amigos. ....

4 ¿Por qué vas al restaurante? ....

H **5** Vivís en Barcelona y es emocionante. ....

H **6** Vais a la sesión de las siete para ver un documental. ....

G

The verbs ***ir*** and ***ser*** in the **preterite tense** are irregular. They have the same form.
Hacer, ***tener*** and ***ver*** are also irregular.

ir (*to go*) **ser** (*to be*)	**hacer** (*to do/make*)	**tener** (*to have*)	**ver** (*to see*)
fui fuiste fue fuimos fuisteis fueron	hice hiciste hizo hicimos hicisteis hicieron	tuve tuviste tuvo tuvimos tuvisteis tuvieron	vi viste vio vimos visteis vieron

Some verbs are irregular in the first person: ***jugué*** (*I played*), ***llegué*** (*I arrived*), ***saqué*** (*I took*).

4 Circle the five verb mistakes made by a student. Then correct the mistakes in the sentences.

Me llamo Noah y el fin de semana pasado yo fue al gimnasio con mi amiga Isla. Luego fuimos al parque, donde yo jugué con mi perro e Isla hice atletismo. ¡Es muy divertido! Sin embargo, Isla y yo no grabaron nada con los móviles porque no tuvo tiempo.

1 ....
2 ....
3 ....
4 ....
5 ....

F 5 Translate these sentences into English.

1 Por la mañana hablé mucho. ....

2 Ayer no fuimos de compras. ....

How should you translate *hace*? Word order?

3 Hace cinco días compré otra entrada. ....

4 Tomamos un café y luego mi novia practicó baloncesto. ....

....

Para can be 'to', 'in order to' or 'for'. Which works best here?

5 Mañana podemos ir al estadio para ver a alguna banda divertida. ....

....

H 6 Translate this paragraph into Spanish on a separate sheet.

Which person of the verb?

Last weekend I stayed at home all day. First my family and I listened to music and then we watched a comedy film. On Sunday morning I read an interesting novel and I shopped online. Later, I did homework. Next weekend we are going to enjoy an exciting day in the shopping centre.

What tense is needed here?

5 ¡Un día fatal!

F Practising different verbs in the preterite tense

1 Complete these sentences with the correct verb in the preterite tense.

1 Ayer .... (*we went*) al estadio, pero .... (*I lost*) a mis amigas.

2 .... (*I played*) al baloncesto y .... (*we won*) el partido.

3 El concierto .... (*it started*) tarde y la cantante .... (*she sang*) mal.

4 El fin de semana pasado .... (*I had*) un día bueno porque mi equipo .... (*it won*).

5 Finalmente, mi amiga no .... (*she bought*) nada porque .... (*she lost*) su móvil.

2 Complete these sentences by translating the words in brackets. Use the verbs in the word bank to help you.

cantó	compró
vi	jugué
ganó	fui
comenzó	perdió
leí	fuimos
hablé	tuve
fue	ganamos
perdí	

1 Tuve un día malo porque .... (*I did not watch TV*).

2 Odié el concierto porque .... (*the music was terrible*).

3 La película de terror .... (*started at eight thirty*).

4 Después fuimos al cine, pero .... (*I lost my phone*).

5 El sábado fuimos a un partido de fútbol, pero .... (*I lost my friends*).

3 Decide if these statements are written in the preterite (P), present (Pr) or future (F).

1 El miércoles pasado fuimos al cine para ver una película nueva. ....

2 La próxima vez vamos a ver algo en casa. ....

3 Siempre voy a los partidos de fútbol con mi madre. ....

4 Escucharon a un grupo nuevo, pero la voz del cantante fue terrible. ....

5 Maite va a ir de compras con sus amigos al centro comercial. ....

G

Remember that the ***yo*** (I) form of regular preterite verbs takes an accent (either **-é** or **-í**).
The ***nosotros*** (we) form of ***-ar*** and ***-ir*** regular verbs has the same ending as in the present tense.
However, ***-er*** verbs change (***comemos*** ⟶ ***comimos***, ***perdemos*** ⟶ ***perdimos***).

-ar	**-er *and* -ir**	
compré – compramos	perdí – perdimos	salí – salimos
caminé – caminamos	comí – comimos	escribí – escribimos

Remember that some verbs have spelling changes in the first person:
jugué – jugamos   llegué – llegamos

Other verbs are irregular:
fui – fuimos   tuve – tuvimos   hice – hicimos

4 Translate these sentences into Spanish.

1 Normally I watch programmes on TV. ....

2 My boyfriend goes to concerts. ....

3 I lost my phone on the train. ....

4 We arrived late last weekend. ....

5 Later we are going to go to a football match. ....

5 ¡Un día fatal!

H Using direct object pronouns

H 1 Draw lines to match up the sentence halves.

1 No tengo móvil porque
2 Normalmente leo muchos libros y
3 Mi padre perdió su cámara y piensa que
4 Mi novia compró tres entradas, pero

a las perdió en el metro.
b lo perdí en el colegio.
c siempre los leo en el tren.
d la perdió en el estadio.

H 2 Circle the correct object pronoun. Then translate each sentence into English.

1 Compré una entrada, pero **lo** / **la** perdí ayer. ....
2 Mandé dos mensajes, pero mi amigo no **los** / **las** leyó. ....
3 Participamos en la competición de baile y **la** / **las** gané. ....
4 No leí el correo electrónico, ya que no **los** / **lo** vi. ....
5 Casi nunca envío las fotos, pero a veces **las** / **los** recibo. ....
6 A mis hemanos les encantan las novelas y **las** / **la** leen en su tiempo libre. ....

H Direct object pronouns replace something or someone that has already been mentioned. **G**
They are positioned directly before the conjugated verb and agree in number with the noun they replace.
Me gustan **las** aplicaciones. → **Las** uso todos los días.

	masculine	feminine
singular	lo	la
plural	los	las

With infinitives, direct object pronouns can be attached to the infinitive or can be placed before the conjugated verb, regardless of the tense used.
No voy a escuchar**lo** / escuchar**la**. No **lo** / **la** voy a escuchar.

H 3 Unjumble the Spanish words to translate the English sentences.

1 las encantan sábados veo y los me películas las. — I love films and I watch them on Saturdays.
....
2 parque lo día y disfruté caminé el otro en. — Another day I walked in the park and I enjoyed it.
....
3 partido amigo tenis jugué de mi lo un perdí con sí pero. — Yes, I played a tennis match with my friend but we lost it.
....
4 mi que libro perdí creo ayer. — I think I lost my book yesterday.
....
5 porque concierto la terrible a fue con fuimos todo perdí mi un cámara pero. — We went to a concert with my camera but everything was terrible because I lost it.
....

H 4 Translate this paragraph into English on a separate sheet.

What nouns do these direct object pronouns replace?

Me gustan los fines de semana. A menudo leo en casa, pero casi nunca veo la tele. Prefiero las novelas porque las encuentro divertidas. Ayer mi hermana perdió su libro en la ciudad cuando fue al centro comercial, pero luego lo vio en la cafetería. Después perdió su móvil en el tren. Mañana tiene que encontrarlo.

Glossary

bold = this word will appear in Higher exams only

a	*to, at, away, on*			
a menudo	*often*			
a veces	*sometimes*			
actividad (f)	*activity*			
aficionado (m)	*fan*			
al	*(to) the (m, sing)*			
amigo (m), amiga (f)	*friend*			
aparato (m)	*device, apparatus*			
aplicación (f)	*application, app*			
argentino	*Argentinian*			
atletismo (m)	*athletics*			
auriculares (mpl)	*headphones, earbuds*			
aventura (f)	*adventure*			
ayer	*yesterday*			
bailar	*(to) dance | dancing*			
baile (m)	*dance*			
baloncesto (m)	*basketball*			
banda (f)	*band*			
beber	*(to) drink | drinking*			
bueno	*good*			
caballo (m)	*horse*			
cadena (f)	*chain, channel*			
canción (f)	*song*			
cantante (mf)	*singer*			
casi	*almost, nearly*			
chatear	*(to) chat (online) | chatting (online)*			
chica (f)	*girl*			
chico (m)	*boy*			
ciclismo (m)	*cycling*			
ciencia ficción (f)	*science fiction*			
cine (m)	*cinema*			
claro	*of course*			
clásico	*classic, classical*			
club (m)	*club, society*			
colgar	*(to) post (online), hang up | posting (online), hanging up*			
comedia (f)	*comedy*			
como	*like, as*			
compra (f)	*shopping, purchase*			
con	*with*			
concierto (m)	*concert*			
conectarse (a Internet)	*(to) connect (online) | connecting (online)*			
contacto (m)	*contact*			
contraseña (f)	*password*			
copa (f)	*cup*			
correo electrónico (m)	*email*			
creer	*(to) think, believe | thinking, believing*			
¿Cuántos/as?	*How many?*			
de	*of, from*			
de vez en cuando	*from time to time*			
del	*of the (m, sing)*			
deporte (m)	*sport*			
descansar	*(to) rest | resting*			
desconocido	*unknown*			
difícil	*difficult*			
disfrutar (de)	*(to) enjoy | enjoying*			
divertido	*funny, amusing*			
documental (m)	*documentary*			
donde	*where (adverb, conjunction)*			
dónde	*where (question)*			
el	*the (m)*			
electrónico	*electronic*			
emocionante	*exciting, touching, moving*			
en	*in, on, at*			
en línea	*online*			

encantar	*(to) love | loving*			
encontrar	*(to) find | finding; (to) run into, be located, feel | running into, being located, feeling*			
entonces	*then, so*			
entrada (f)	*entrance, admission ticket*			
enviar	*(to) send | sending*			
equipo (m)	*team, equipment*			
es	*(she, he, it, one) is | **(you (sing formal)) are***			
escuchar	*(to) listen | listening*			
estadio (m)	*stadium*			
estar	*(to) be | being*			
estoy	*(I) am | (I) am being*			
fácil	*easy*			
favorito	*favourite*			
finalmente	*finally*			
foto (f)	*photo*			
fue	*(she, he, it, one) went | (you (sing formal)) went | (she, he, it, one) was | (you (sing formal)) were*			
fueron	*(they) went | (you (pl formal)) went | they were | (you (pl formal)) were*			
fui	*(I) went | (I) was*			
fuimos	*(we) went | (we) were*			
fuiste	*(you (sing informal)) went | (you (sing informal)) were*			
fuisteis	*(you (pl informal)) went | (you (pl informal)) were*			
fútbol (m)	*football*			
gira (f)	*tour*			
grabar	*(to) record, film | recording, filming*			
gustar	*(to) like, be pleasing to | liking, being pleasing to*			
hablar	*(to) speak | speaking*			
hacer	*(to) do, make | doing, making*			
hasta	*until, up to*			
hice	*(I) did, made*			
imagen (f)	*image, picture*			
increíble	*incredible, unbelievable*			
información (f)	*information*			
interesante	*interesting*			
interesar	*(to) interest, be of interest | interesting, being of interest*			
Internet (m)	*Internet*			
ir de compras	*(to) go shopping | going shopping*			
juega (a), ¡juega (a)!	*(she, he, it, one) plays | (she, he, it, one) is playing | (you (sing formal)) play | (you (sing formal)) are playing | Play! (you (sing informal))*			
juegan (a)	*(they) play | (they) are playing*			
juegas (a)	*(you) play | (you) are playing*			
juego (a)	*(I) play | (I) am playing*			
jugador (m), jugadora (f)	*player*			
jugar (a)	*(to) play | playing*			
la	*the (f)*			
las	*the (fpl)*			
lector (m), lectora (f)	*reader*			
leer	*(to) read | reading*			
libro (m)	*book*			
luego	*later | afterwards*			
malo	*bad*			
mandar	*(to) send | sending*			
mensaje (m)	*message*			
mi	*my*			
miembro (m)	*member*			

montar	*(to) ride | riding*
móvil (m)	*mobile phone*
mucho	*much, many, a lot of*
música (f)	*music*
pop (m), música pop (f)	*pop*
musical (m)	*musical*
muy	*very*
nada, (no) nada	*nothing, anything (after negative verb)*
natación (f)	*swimming*
necesario	*necessary*
nombre (m)	*name*
normalmente	*normally*
noticias (fpl)	*news*
novela (f)	*novel*
nuevo	*new*
nunca, (no) nunca	*never*
o/u	*or*
odiar	*(to) hate | hating*
ordenador (portátil) (m)	*(laptop) computer*
otro	*other, another*
pantalla (f)	*screen*
parque (m)	*park*
partido (m)	*match (sports), (political) party*
pasado	*last, past*
pasar	*(to) spend (time), pass by, happen | spending (time), passing by, happening*
pasatiempo (m)	*leisure activity, hobby*
pasión (f)	*passion*
película (f)	*film*
peligroso	*dangerous*
pensar (de)	*(to) think (of/about) | thinking (of/about)*
pero	*but*
persona (f)	*person*
poder	*(to) be able to, can | being able to*
por qué	*why*
porque	*because*
preferir	*(to) prefer | preferring*
primero	*firstly*
privado	*private*
programa (m)	*show (TV, radio), programme (activity, plan)*
próximo	*next*
que	*who, that, which (subj)*
que	*than, that (subj)*
¿Qué?	*What?*
quedar; quedarse	*(to) meet up | meeting up; (to) stay | staying*
querer	*(to) want, love | wanting, loving*
recibir	*(to) receive, welcome | receiving, welcoming*
relajante	*relaxing*
restaurante (m)	*restaurant*
revista (f)	*magazine*
ritmo (m)	*rhythm*
rock (m)	*rock (music)*
salir	*(to) leave, depart, go out | leaving, departing, going out*
seguidor (m), seguidora (f)	*follower*
serie (f)	*series*
sesión (f)	*session*
si	*if, whether*
sí	*yes*
siempre	*always, forever*
sois	*(you (pl informal)) are*

son	*(they) are | (they) have been | (you (pl formal)) are | it is (+ time)*
sonido (m)	*sound*
soy	*(I) am*
su	*his, her, its, one's, your (formal), their*
también	*also*
tarde	*late*
tele(visión) (f)	*TV*
tenis (m)	*tennis*
terrible	*terrible*
terror (m)	*terror, horror*
tiempo (m)	*time, weather*
todo	*all, the whole (+ noun)*
todo	*everything, all*
todos	*everyone, all of them*
tomar	*(to) take, have (drink, food) | taking, having*
tu	*your (sing, informal)*
tuve; tuve que	*(I) had; (I) had to*
un	*a/an (m)*
una	*a/an (f)*
usar	*(to) use | using*
usuario (m), usuaria (f)	*user*
utilizar	*(to) use | using*
va; **se va (de)**	*(she, he, it, one) goes | (she, he, it, one) is going | (you (sing formal)) go | (you (sing formal)) are going | **(she, he, it, one) leaves | (she, he, it, one) is leaving | (you (sing formal)) leave | (you (sing formal)) are leaving***
vais; **os vais (de)**	*(you (pl informal)) go | (you (pl informal)) are going | **(you (pl informal)) leave | (you (pl informal)) are leaving***
vamos; **nos vamos (de)**	*(we) go | (we) are going | **(we) leave | (we) are leaving***
van; **se van (de)**	*(they) go | (they) are going | (you (pl formal)) go | (you (pl formal)) are going | **(they) leave | (they) are leaving | (you (pl formal)) leave | (you (pl formal)) are leaving***
vas; **te vas (de)**	*(you (sing informal)) go | (you (sing informal)) are going | **(you (sing informal)) leave | (you (sing informal)) are leaving***
venir	*(to) come | coming*
ver	*(to) see, watch | seeing, watching*
vídeo (m)	*video*
videoconsola (f)	*games console*
virtual	*virtual*
vóleibol (m)	*volleyball*
voy; **me voy (de)**	*(I) go | (I) am going | **(I) leave | (I) am leaving***
web (f)	*Internet, web*
yo	*I (subj)*

Zona de cultura ¡Descubre Andalucía!

Using *me gusta(n) / me gustaría* + infinitive

G

The verb **gustar** changes depending on if the thing you like is singular or plural.

singular		plural	
Me gusta *el sol.*	I like the sun.	*No **me gustan** los caballos.*	I don't like horses.
Me gusta *mucho la cultura.*	I really like the culture.	***Me gustan*** *los turistas.*	I like tourists.

1 Circle the correct verb to complete each sentence.

1 Me **gusta** / **gustan** el transporte público.
2 Me **gusta** / **gustan** los barcos.
3 ¿Te **gusta** / **gustan** los animales?
4 Me **gusta** / **gustan** el turismo.
5 No me **gusta** / **gustan** las vistas de la ciudad.
6 Me **encanta** / **encantan** los espectáculos de flamenco.

2 Complete the sentences using the words in the box. Then complete the translations.

tranquilos	hay
hermosa	muchos
sol	turistas
izquierda	foto
campo	

1 En la ...foto... hay muchas casas y llueve.
In the photo there are many ...houses and it's raining...
2 A la derecha ...hay... una playa y muchos edificios.
On the right there is ...a beach ~~and~~ and lots of building...
3 A la ...izquierda... hay un río y un pueblo.
On the left there is ...a river and a town...
4 La chica está en el ...campo... y hace mucho ...sol...
The girl is in the ...countryside and it's very sunny...
H 5 La región atrae a muchos ...turistas... porque los valles son ...~~hermosa~~ tranquilos
The region attracts ...tourists because the valleys are calm...
H 6 También hay ...muchos... árboles y la arena es ...hermosa...
There are also ...lots of trees and the area is beautifull...

3 Translate these sentences into Spanish.

1 I like the sea because it is calm. ...Me gusta el mar porque es calmo...
2 I don't like historic buildings. ...No me gusta los edificios historicos...
3 When it is hot, I like beaches. ...Cuando esta calor, me gustas las playas...
H 4 I love the big trees and the old houses.
...Me encanta los arboles y las casas vejas...
H 5 According to a survey, many tourists visit the valley.
...De Acuerdo con una encuesta, muchos turistas visitan el valle...

4 Fill in the missing words in these questions.

1 Where would you like to go? – ¿Dónde gustarias ir?

2 Would you like to visit the north of Spain? – ¿Te gustariá el norte de España?

3 Would you like to see a historic city? – ¿Gustarias una ciudad histórica?

4 Would you like to go horse riding? – Gustarias montar a caballo

> **G** When you want to say what you would like to do, use the conditional tense of ***gustar*** with an infinitive. Use ***encantar*** in the same way.
>
> ***Me gustaría** visitar la costa.* — I **would like** to visit the coast.
>
> ***Me encantaría** caminar por el centro.* — I **would love** to walk through the (town) centre.

H 5 Unjumble the Spanish words to write sentences.

1 mi con gustaría familia campo ir Me al Me gustariá ir con mi samilia al campo

2 un flamenco Me de ver gustaría espectáculo Me gustariá ver un espectaculo de slamenco

3 el me centro No gustaría visitar histórico No me gustaria visitar el centro historico

4 tomar natación Me el hacer gustaría sol y Me gustaría tomar ~~natacion~~ sol y hacer natación

F 6 Translate these sentences into Spanish.

1 I don't like forests. No me gustan los bosques

2 In the photo there is a river. ~~N~~ En la soto hay un rio

3 On the right there are beautiful views. A la derecha hay vistas hermosas

Which verb is used for location? *Ser* or *estar*? estar

4 They are in an old town. Estan en una pueblo vejo

5 I would like to go to the beach. Me gustaría ir a la playa

How do you translate this verb with weather expressions?

H 7 Translate this paragraph into English.

En la foto hay mucha gente en una bonita playa. A la izquierda hay muchos árboles verdes y al fondo hay agua. En el centro una familia está en un barco pequeño en el mar. Creo que hace mucho calor. Me gustaría ir a la costa para tomar el sol y hacer turismo.

In the photo there are lots os people at a pretty beach. To the left there are lots os green trees and in the backgrand there's water. In the middle ~~there is a~~ samily is on a small boat on the sea. I think it is very sunny. I wald like to go to the coast to sunbathe and go sight seeing.

1 En ruta

Using comparatives • Using *se puede(n)* + infinitive

1 Write the correct letter in the box to match up the questions with the answers.

1 ¿Con quién te gustaría viajar? [c]

2 ¿Adónde te gustaría ir de vacaciones? [a]

3 ¿Cómo te gustaría viajar? [e]

4 ¿Cuándo te gustaría ir? [b]

5 ¿Qué tipo de destino te gustaría visitar? [d]

a Me gustaría ir de vacaciones a Asia.

b En verano es más fácil.

c Pues, quisiera viajar sola.

d Me gustaría visitar el campo o la montaña.

e Prefiero viajar en autobús porque es barato.

2 Write the English for each infinitive. Then use it in a sentence with *me gustaría* or *quisiera*.

1 viajar — to travel — Quisiera viajar en tren o en coche.

2 pasear — to go sor a walk — Gustaria de passear en

3 disfrutar de — to enjoy — Gustaria disfrutar la comida food

H 4 hacer turismo — to go sightseeing — Quiseria hacer turismo en Berlin

H 5 apreciar — to appreciate — Gustaria de apreciar b ~~moseeo~~ museo de arte

3 Translate the sentences using the table.

<table>
<tr><td rowspan="3">(No) Me gustaría

(No) Quisiera</td><td rowspan="3">viajar en
ir en</td><td rowspan="3">autobús
avión
barco
coche
metro
tren</td><td rowspan="3">porque es</td><td>más
menos</td><td rowspan="2">barato
caro
cómodo
difícil
lento
rápido
seguro</td><td>que</td><td>el avión / el barco.</td></tr>
<tr><td>tan</td><td>como</td><td>ir en tren / en coche.</td></tr>
<tr><td colspan="2">mejor
peor</td><td>que</td><td>viajar en autobús / en metro.</td></tr>
</table>

1 I would not like to travel by bus because it is slower than going by car.

No gustaria viajar de autobus porque es más lento que ~~via~~ ir en coche

2 I would not like to go by boat because it is less safe than going by train.

No me gustaria ir de barco porque es menos seguro ~~de~~ que ir de tren

3 I would like to go by plane because it is better than going by car.

Gustaria ir de avion porque es mejor ~~de~~ que ir de coche

4 I would not like to travel by underground because it is worse than the train.

No me gustaria ir en metro porque es peor que viajar en tren.

4 Complete each sentence with the correct infinitive from the box.

disfrutar	ir	viajar	dormir	visitar	tomar

1 Se puede tomar el sol.
2 Se puede visitar la ciudad.
3 Se puede ir viajar en barco.
4 Se puede dormir durante el vuelo.
5 Se puede disfrutar del buen clima.
6 Se puede ir de compras.

G
Use ***se puede*** to say 'you/one can'. It is always followed by the infinitive.

Se puede *coger el metro.*	**You can** catch the underground.
Se puede *ver la estación.*	**You can** see the station.
Se puede *visitar el pueblo.*	**You can** visit the town.

H 5 Complete each sentence with the correct form of *se puede / se pueden*.

1 Se pueden visitar los monumentos.
2 También se puede apreciar la cultura. lo centro
3 Se puede descubrir el castillo situado en la ciudad.
4 Se pueden viajar por paisajes bonitos.

G
H *Se puede* changes when the infinitive is followed by a plural noun, becoming ***se pueden***.

Se puede *visitar el jardín.*	You can visit the garden.
Se pueden *probar platos locales.*	You can try local dishes.

Where the infinitive is not followed immediately by the noun, use ***se puede***.

Se puede *pasear por las playas.*	You can walk on the beaches.

F 6 Translate these sentences into English.

1 Quisiera ver la carta. I would like to see the menu
2 El autobús es más cómodo. The bus is more comfartble
3 Me gustaría ir a pie. I would like to go on foot

Use one word to translate this.

4 Cuando tengo equipaje, el coche es más fácil. When I have baggage, the car is easier
5 Se puede disfrutar del buen clima en el campo. You can enjoy the good weather in the countryside

H 7 Translate this paragraph into Spanish.

Translate this using the verb *tardar* with *mucho*.

I would like to go on holiday to the coast. In spring you can enjoy good weather. I would like to travel by train because it is more comfortable for long distance, although it takes a very long time. Last year I travelled by plane. I also would like to go with a group of friends and try typical dishes.

Me gustaria ir de vaccaciones a la costa. En la primavera puedes disfrutar del ~~tempo~~ buen tempo. ~~Me~~ Gustaria de ~~ir~~ viajar de tren porque es mas comfortavle para distancias longes, pero ~~demora~~ tarda mucho tiempo. Lo año pasado, viaje de avion. Tambien ~~quiero~~ me gustaria ir con un grupo de amigos y probar los platos tipicos.

2 La cultura en la calle

Module 2
Student Book pp. 34–35

- F Using *hay* and *hay que*
- F Using extended sentences with 'if'

1 Write the correct letter in the box to match up the sentence halves.

1 Si te interesa la historia, ☐
2 Si te gusta la naturaleza, ☐
3 Si te gusta tirar cosas, ☐
4 Si te interesa la comida, ☐
5 Si te gustan los espectáculos, ☐

a hay que celebrar la Tomatina en agosto.
b hay que ver los bailes típicos.
c hay que visitar el museo.
d hay que probar las tapas. ¡Buen provecho!
e hay que ir al parque.

2 Underline the English parts in this tangled text. Then rewrite the whole text in Spanish underneath.

Si you like la música, hay que participate en las fiestas de los towns in el sur de Spain. Puedes eat paella y ver flamenco shows. There are mucha gente on the streets y always es quite divertido. I recommend these local festivals porque son fiestas culturales y exciting para todos los gustos.

....

....

....

....

G

Use ***hay*** to say 'there is' or 'there are'. It is followed by a noun.
Use ***hay que*** to say 'you must'. It is followed by an infinitive.

Hay *una feria increíble.*	**There is** an incredible fair.
Hay que *ver las Fallas en marzo.*	**You must** see the Fallas in March.

3 Circle the correct verb structure to complete each sentence.

1 En invierno **hay** / **hay que** muchos eventos especiales.
2 En primavera **hay** / **hay que** ir a las fiestas populares.
3 En verano **hay** / **hay que** participar en bailes en la calle.
4 En otoño **hay** / **hay que** una noche increíble durante la feria.

4 Translate these sentences into Spanish.

1 I recommend the festival. ....
2 In spring there are many shows. ....
3 I would like a table for six people. ....

Translate this using *hay que* + infinitive.

4 If you like paella, you must go to a fair. ....
5 We are going to eat a sandwich or an omelette. ....

2 La cultura en la calle

- **H** Using the superlative
- **H** Using 'if' clauses with the present tense

H 1 Complete each sentence by translating the missing words.

1 Si te gustan .... (*fireworks*), hay que .... (*visit*) las Fallas de Valencia.

2 Hay que .... (*go*) a la feria si quieres .... (*enjoy*) de la vida cultural.

3 Si te interesan .... (*customs*) locales, hay que .... (*travel*) a Latinoamérica.

4 Hay que .... (*participate*) en festivales si te gusta .... (*adventure*).

5 Si te encantan los festivales .... (*well-known*), hay que descubrir .... (*processions*) famosos.

G

H Use the **superlative** to talk about the best, the worst, the biggest, etc. Remember that the adjective needs to agree with the noun.

*Quizás **el** plato **más** popular es la paella.*	Perhaps the **most** popular dish is paella.
***La** tradición **menos** conocida es el baile.*	The **least** well-known tradition is the dance.

Note these irregular superlatives:

el/la/los/las	*mejor(es)*	*peores*	*mayor(es)*	*menor(es)*
the	best	worst	biggest	smallest

H 2 Circle the correct adjective to complete each superlative.

1 ¿Cuál es la fiesta más **conocido / conocida / conocidos / conocidas**?

2 Mi amigo dice que el desfile es la parte más **tradicional / tradicionales**.

3 Los platos son ricos y son los más **típico / típica / típicos / típicas** de la región.

4 Creo que las tapas son las **mejor / mejores** de toda la ciudad.

5 El público dentro de la plaza es el más **grande / grandes**.

H 3 Use these nouns and adjectives to create four superlative sentences about a festival trip.

La música, El ruido, El viaje, La comida, Las costumbres

mayor(es), hermoso/a(s), rico/a(s), barato/a(s), importante(s), mejor(es), típico/a(s)

1 ....

2 ....

3 ....

4 ....

H 4 Translate this paragraph into English on a separate sheet.

Don't translate this word separately. It is translated with the verb *disfrutar*.

Hay muchas fiestas donde se puede disfrutar de los desfiles. Delante de los edificios se pueden ver miles de personas en las calles. También se puede escuchar la mejor música. Si te gusta el ruido y quieres divertirte, hay que ir. Cada año mi familia y yo participamos, y comemos muy bien. Los platos más pequeños son los más ricos.

3 Mis últimas vacaciones

F Practising the 'I' and 'we' forms of preterite tense verbs

1 Write the correct letter to match up the weather expressions to the correct symbols.

1 Por la mañana hizo sol. ☐

2 Por la tarde hizo frío. ☐

3 Por la noche hizo viento. ☐

4 Ayer nevó. ☐

5 Hace una semana llovió. ☐

a

b

c

d

e

2 Complete the table with the correct verb forms.

English	Infinitive	I (*yo*) – preterite	We (*nosotros*) – preterite
to visit	visitar	*visité*	visitamos
	pasar		pasamos
	hacer	hice	
	ver	vi	
	ir		fuimos
	dejar		dejamos
	perder	perdí	
	romper		rompimos

G

Verbs in the 'I' and 'we' form in the preterite are very useful when speaking or writing about past activities. Remember, the 'we' form will always end in ***-mos***.

*Pas**é** una semana en Valencia.* — I spent a week in Valencia.

*Mi familia y yo celebra**mos** la Nochevieja allí.* — My family and I celebrated New Year's Eve there.

3 Complete these sentences by translating the verbs in brackets.

1 .... (*I went*) al aeropuerto, pero .... (*I lost*) mi pasaporte allí.

2 .... (*We spent*) tres noches en un hotel y .... (*we visited*) el castillo.

3 Mis amigos y yo .... (*we went*) de vacaciones y .... (*I bought*) unos recuerdos.

4 .... (*I travelled*) en autobús al puerto, pero .... (*I lost*) mis llaves.

5 .... (*We went*) a un restaurante, pero .... (*I ate*) algo malo.

4 Translate these sentences into English.

1 Fui de viaje con mi familia. ....

2 Al día siguiente visitamos el museo. ....

How do we translate *un* or *una* when it is plural?

3 Vimos unos recuerdos bonitos en la playa. ....

4 Luego tomé un helado porque hizo mucho sol. ....

5 El último día rompí mi cámara en el tren y fue terrible. ....

....

3 Mis últimas vacaciones

H Using *acabar de* + infinitive

H 1 Unjumble the Spanish words to translate the English questions.

1 How was your last holiday? *¿tus últimas tal vacaciones qué?*

....

2 What was the weather like the first day? *¿tiempo el hizo día qué primer?*

....

3 What did you do in the afternoon? *¿qué por tarde hiciste la?*

....

4 What was the best thing about your holiday? *¿de lo tus fue mejor vacaciones qué?*

....

5 What was the worst thing? *¿peor fue qué lo?*

....

G

H Use ***acabar de*** + infinitive to say that you have just done something. You use it in the present tense in Spanish, even though the English translation is in the past tense.

***Acabamos de** regresar de nuestras vacaciones.* **We have just** returned from our holidays.

***Acaban de** comprar unos recuerdos.* **They have just** bought some souvenirs.

H 2 Complete each sentence with the correct form of *acabar de* + infinitive.

1 Yo .... (*visit*) un museo pequeño cerca de la costa.

2 Khalid .... (*see*) unos jardines únicos.

3 Mi novia .... (*find*) unos lugares especiales.

4 Mis hermanos .... (*travel all over*) el hermoso centro de la ciudad.

H 3 Underline the English parts in this tangled text. Then rewrite the whole text in Spanish.

I have just volver de Asia donde I spent tres semanas with my family. We travelled mucho en coche y fue quite boring. The best thing de mi visita fue cuando we visited un mercado enorme. Compré some souvenirs para mi boyfriend. Hizo cold y it rained mucho pero lo peor was when dejé my bag in the station.

....

....

....

H 4 Translate this paragraph into Spanish.

Translate this whole phrase using *encantar* in the preterite.

My friends and I just visited the port where we spent three days. We loved it because you can do lots there, but the first day I ate something bad and I lost my card. The worst thing was when I broke my camera. It also was windy and it rained.

....

....

....

4 ¿Dónde te quedaste?

Using the imperfect tense

1 Write the English for these hotel facilities.

1 habitaciones dobles ....

2 habitaciones individuales ....

3 habitaciones con dos camas ....

4 vistas al mar ....

5 desayuno incluido ....

6 piscina al aire libre gratuita ....

G

The **imperfect tense** is used to describe things in the past:

*El hotel **tenía** unas habitaciones caras.*	The hotel **had** some expensive rooms.
***Era** moderno y barato.*	**It was** modern and cheap.
***Había** mucho ruido durante el día.*	**There was** a lot of noise during the day.

Estar in the imperfect is used for describing a location or temporary state in the past:

*La ventana **estaba** rota.*	The window **was** broken.
*El camping **estaba** cerca del río.*	The campsite **was** near the river.

2 Draw lines to match up the sentence halves.

1 La casa no tenía	a piscina, pero era muy moderna.
2 El baño del camping	b estaba muy limpia.
3 Nos quedamos en una casa	c bonita, pero la ventana estaba rota.
4 La piscina del hotel	d barato, pero había mucho ruido.
5 El desayuno era muy	e estaba muy sucio.

3 Circle the correct verbs to complete the text.

El verano pasado **me quedo** / **me quedé** en un camping en el campo. El camping **era** / **tenía** enorme y **estaba** / **había** lejos de la ciudad. No **era** / **tenía** piscina e **hice** / **hizo** mucho sol. En el camping **había** / **estaba** un restaurante, pero las mesas **estaban** / **tenían** rotas, y la cocina **estaba** / **era** demasiado pequeña.

4 Complete the sentences using the words in the box. There are more words than gaps.

vacía baño habitación incluido | H alojamiento H dueño H rota H estrellas

1 Quisiera reservar una .... individual para dos noches.

2 Perdón, señor, pero la habitación no está ....

3 El desayuno es a las siete y está ....

H 4 Me alojé en un hotel de cinco ....

H 5 La luz estaba .... y no había ascensor.

H 6 El .... no tenía ni cocina ni ascensor.

H 5 Change this present tense text into the past.

Voy a un hotel lindo. Lo bueno es que el hotel no es caro y es posible cargar el coche eléctrico allí. Lo malo es que no tiene ni jardín ni gimnasio y tampoco hay piscina. Por un lado, las habitaciones son amplias, pero, por otro lado, los ascensores no funcionan. En el restaurante los tenedores y los vasos están sucios.

G

H The imperfect forms of ***-er*** and ***-ir*** verbs share the same endings.

	-ar	-er/-ir
(yo)	est**aba**	ten**ía**
(tú)	est**abas**	ten**ías**
(él/ella/usted)	est**aba**	ten**ía**
(nosotros/as)	est**ábamos**	ten**íamos**
(vosotros/as)	est**abais**	ten**íais**
(ellos/as/ustedes)	est**aban**	ten**ían**

Fui a un hotel lindo. ....

....

....

....

F 6 Translate these sentences into Spanish.

1 I would like a room for five nights.

....

2 I stayed at a campsite.

....

What tense do you use for past descriptions and what verb for describing a temporary state?

3 The bed was broken and there was no pool.

....

4 I did not like the garden because it was dirty.

....

5 The breakfast was expensive but there were not many people.

....

H 7 Translate this paragraph into English.

Translate this as 'us'. Think about the word order of this part of the sentence.

No quiero quejarme, pero muchos alojamientos no son buenos. Mi pareja y yo alquilamos una casa y tuvimos muchos problemas, y la dueña no nos ayudó. La luz no funcionaba, no había ni jardín ni vistas del mar, y tampoco estaba cerca de la playa. Además, había demasiado ruido de la calle.

....

....

....

....

5 Mi aventura por Latinoamérica

F Using three different time frames

1 Translate the sentences using words and phrases from the grid.

ayer	fui	voy a comprar	series en mi tableta
normalmente	voy	llego	al extranjero
siempre	viajo	voy a viajar	cuadros de artistas famosos
el fin de semana pasado	voy a llegar	vi	el domingo por la tarde
en las vacaciones	voy a ir	compro	un espectáculo
la próxima semana	veo	compré	al festival del Día de los Muertos
todos los días	voy a hacer	viajé	comida tradicional
el verano pasado	llegamos	vimos	mi silla de ruedas nueva

1 I normally buy traditional food. ....

2 Last weekend I bought my new wheelchair. ....

3 Every day I watch series on my tablet. ....

4 Next week I am going to go to the Day of the Dead festival.

....

5 On holiday we saw famous artists' paintings. ....

2 Fill in the gaps with an appropriate verb. Use the verbs in the box from exercise 1.

1 El último día mis amigos y yo .... al aeropuerto a las siete.

2 Ayer fui al centro comercial y .... regalos para mi familia.

3 Creo que mañana .... natación porque hace buen tiempo.

4 Voy al festival del Día de los Muertos y .... flores para los muertos.

G

Use different tenses to express different time frames.

Use the **present** to say what you do or normally do.
Descanso *en casa y siempre* ***leo*** *mucho.*
I **rest** at home and I always **read** a lot.

Use the **preterite** to talk about what you did, past weather and to give opinions in the past.
Fui *a un restaurante donde la cuenta* ***estuvo*** *bien de precio.*
I **went** to a restaurant where the bill **was** a good price.

Use the **near future** to talk about what you are going to do.
Voy a conocer *a mucha gente.*
I am going to meet a lot of people.

3 Write the correct tense of each verb in brackets to complete the sentences.

1 Ayer fui al parque e .... (*hacer*) deporte con mis amigos.

2 Mañana mi hermana y yo .... (*tomar*) el sol en la playa.

3 Normalmente mi padre no .... (*ir*) al estadio para ver los partidos.

4 El mes pasado fui al extranjero y .... (*aprender*) mucho.

4 Translate these sentences into English.

1 En verano siempre hago ciclismo. ....

2 Disfrutamos al máximo las rutas. ....

3 Siempre es un placer conocer a gente. ....

What tense follows this time expression?

4 Ayer participamos en un viaje para personas con discapacidad.

....

5 Mañana vamos a alquilar un barco para ver la bonita costa.

....

H 1 Underline the errors in the English translations. Then write the correct translations.

1 En verano suelo salir con mis amigos.
In spring I usually go out with my siblings. ....

2 Hace tres años vi una exposición de arte.
Three days ago we saw an art exhibition. ....

3 Lo mejor fue cuando ganamos el premio.
The best thing was when I won a competition. ....

4 Al día siguiente hicimos una excursión en coche.
The day before we went on an outing by coach. ....

5 Por supuesto, compré muchas cosas tradicionales.
Of course I bought some traditional souvenirs. ....

H 2 Circle the correct verb to complete each sentence.

1 El próximo año Maylin no **se quemó / se quema / va a quemarse** si hace sol.

2 Después de la llegada del vuelo ayer, mucha gente **sale / va a salir / salió** del aeropuerto.

3 En las vacaciones suelo **tener / tengo / tenía** una maleta pequeña.

4 Todos los días la gente suele molestarme cuando **viajé / viajo / voy a viajar** en autobús.

5 Mañana **vamos a ver / vemos a ver / vimos a ver** las flores que representan el amor y el respeto.

G

H To say what you tend to do or usually do, you can use **soler** + infinitive.

Suelo *comprar algo en el mercado los sábados.*

I usually buy something at the market on Saturdays

Soler is a stem-changing verb:

suelo	*suele*	*soléis*
sueles	*solemos*	*suelen*

H 3 Write the question for each answer.

1

El próximo año voy a hacer turismo con mi familia.

2

Lo peor de mis vacaciones fue cuando no encontré una silla libre en el jardín del hotel.

3

El año pasado fui de vacaciones a un pueblo bonito cerca de una playa vacía.

4

El último día fui a la piscina al aire libre, donde tomé el sol.

H 4 Translate this paragraph into Spanish.

We don't tend to go abroad in the holidays. We normally stay at home as flights are quite expensive. Two weeks ago I went to the capital and I decided to try some new things. The best thing was when I saw a flamenco show. Next year we are going to rent a house.

....

....

....

bold = this word will appear in Higher exams only

acabar; acabar de (+ infinitive)	*(to) finish | finishing; (to) have just + pp*			
aeropuerto (m)	*airport*			
algo	*something*			
alojamiento (m)	*accommodation*			
alojarse	*(to) stay (accommodation) | staying (accommodation)*			
alquilar	*(to) rent, hire | renting, hiring*			
amplio	*large, wide, loose*			
antiguo	*former, antique, old*			
apreciar	*(to) appreciate | appreciating*			
aprovechar	*(to) take advantage of, make the most of | taking advantage of, making the most of*			
árbol (m)	*tree*			
arena (f)	*sand*			
ascensor (m)	*lift*			
atraer	*(to) attract | attracting*			
aunque	*although*			
autobús (m), bus (m)	*bus*			
avión (m)	*plane*			
baño (m)	*bathroom, bath, swim*			
barato	*cheap*			
barco (m)	*boat , ship*			
bastante	*rather, quite, enough*			
bocadillo (m)	*sandwich*			
bonito	*beautiful, nice*			
buen	*good (before singular masculine noun)*			
¡buen provecho!	*enjoy your meal!*			
calor (m)	*heat, warmth, hot*			
cama (f)	*bed*			
cámara (f)	*camera*			
camping (m)	*camping, camp site*			
campo (m)	*countryside, field*			
cargar	*(to) charge | charging*			
caro	*expensive*			
carta (f)	*menu, letter, (playing) card*			
celebrar	*(to) celebrate | celebrating*			
centro (m)	*centre, downtown*			
cerca (de)	*close, near*			
clima (m)	*climate*			
coche (m)	*car*			
coger	*(to) take, catch | taking, catching*			
cómo	*how*			
cómodo	*comfortable*			
comprar	*(to) buy | buying*			
conocido	*known, well-known*			
costa (f)	*coast*			
costumbre (f)	*habit, custom, tradition*			
cuadro (m)	*painting*			
(¿)cuál(es)(?)	*which(?), what(?) (m,f)(pl)*			
cuando	*when*			
cuándo	*when*			
cuenta (f)	*bill, account*			
cultura (f)	*culture*			
cultural	*cultural*			
delante (de)	*(in) front (of)*			
dentro; dentro de	*inside; within, inside*			
derecha (f)	*right, right hand*			
desayuno (m)	*breakfast*			
descubrir	*(to) discover | discovering*			
desfile (m)	*parade*			
destino (m)	*destination*			
El Día de los Muertos (m)	*Day of the Dead*			

discapacidad (f); con discapacidad	*disability; disabled*
distancia (f)	*distance*
doble	*double*
dueño (m), dueña (f)	*owner, landlord*
durante	*during*
enorme	*enormous, vast*
equipaje (m)	*luggage*
especial	*special*
espectáculo (m)	*show (e.g. theatre)*
está	*(she, he, it, one) is | is being | (you (sing formal)) are | are being*
estación (f)	*season, station (train, bus...)*
estrella (f)	*star*
extranjero	*foreign*
Las Fallas (de Valencia) (fpl)	*The Fallas festival*
feria (f)	*fair, festival*
festival (m)	*festival*
fiesta (f)	*party, bank holiday, festival*
flamenco (m)	*flamenco (dance | music)*
frío	*cold*
frío (m)	*cold*
fuego (m)	*fire*
funcionar	*(to) work | working*
gente (f)	*people*
grande	*big, large (m, f) (post-noun)*
gratuito	*free*
grupo (m)	*group, band*
gusto (m)	*pleasure, taste*
había	*there was | there were | there used to be*
habitación (f)	*room, bedroom*
hacer turismo	*(to) sightsee | sightseeing*
hay	*there is | there are*
hay que	*you must (general), one must*
hermoso	*beautiful*
hizo	*(she, he, it, one) did, made | (you (sing formal)) did, made*
hotel (m)	*hotel*
incluido	*included, inclusive of*
individual	*single (room, bed), individual*
ir(se) de vacaciones	*(to) go on holiday | going on holiday*
izquierda (f)	*left*
jardín (m)	*garden*
largo	*long*
lento	*slow*
libre	*free, vacant*
limpio	*clean*
lindo	*beautiful*
llave (f)	*key*
llegada (f)	*arrival*
llover	*(to) rain | raining*
lo (+ adjective, e.g. bueno)	*the (adjective, e.g. good) thing*
luz (f)	*light*
mal	*bad (m) (pre-noun), badly*
maleta (f)	*suitcase*
mar (m)	*sea*
máximo	*maximum*
me/te/le gustaría	*(I, you, she, he, it, you (sing formal)) would like (informal)*
mejor	*better | **best***
el mejor, la mejor, los mejores, las mejores	*the best (m, f, mpl, fpl)*
el menor, la menor, los menores, las menores	*the youngest*
menos; menos (...que)	*less; less (... than)*

menos; menos (...que)	*less, fewer; less (...than), fewer (...than)*
mesa (f)	*table,* ***board***
moderno	*modern*
molestar	*(to) annoy | annoying*
muerto	*dead*
nevar	*(to) snow | snowing*
(no) ni...(ni)...	*nor, or (after negative verb) neither...nor...*
noche (f)	*night, evening*
Nochevieja (f)	*New Year's Eve*
nuestro, nuestra, nuestros, nuestras	*ours (m, f, mpl, fpl)*
paella (f)	*paella*
pareja (f)	*partner, couple*
participar	*(to) participate | participating*
pasaporte (m)	*passport*
peor	*worse,* ***worst***
el peor, la peor, los peores, las peores	*the worst*
pequeño	*small, little, young*
perdón	*(I am) sorry*
piscina (f)	*swimming pool*
placer (m)	*pleasure, amusement*
plato (m)	*plate, dish, course*
playa (f)	*beach*
popular	*popular*
por supuesto	*indeed, of course*
posible	*possible*
público	*public*
público (m)	*public, audience*
puerto (m)	*port, harbour*
quejarse	*(to) complain | complaining*
quemar(se)	*(to) burn (oneself) | burning (oneself)*
(¿)quién(es)(?)	*who(?) (m,f)(pl)*
quisiera	*(I) would like (formal)*
quizá, quizás	*perhaps, maybe*
rápido	*fast, quick*
recomendar	*(to) recommend | recommending*
recorrer	*(to) travel all over | travelling all over*
recuerdo (m)	*souvenir, memory*
regresar	*(to) return | returning*
representar	*(to) represent, play the role of | representing, playing the role of*
reservar	*(to) reserve, book | reserving, booking*
rico	*tasty, rich*
roto	*broken*
ruido (m)	*noise*
ruta (f)	*route*
se puede	*you can (general), one can*
según	*according to*
señor	*Mr, sir*
siguiente	*next, following*
silla (f)	*chair, seat*
silla de ruedas (f)	*wheelchair*
situar; situarse	*to locate | locating; (to) be located | being located*
sol (m)	*sun, sunny*
soler	*(to) usually do | usually doing*
sucio	*dirty*
tableta (f)	*tablet*
(no) tampoco	*neither, nor, either (after negative verb)*
tan...como	*as...as*
tapas (fpl)	*tapas*
tardar	*(to) delay, take long | delaying, taking long*
tarjeta (f)	*card, credit card*

tenedor (m)	*fork*
tenía; tenía que	*(I) had | used to have | was having | (she, he, it, one) had | used to have | was having | (you (sing formal)) had | used to have | were having; (I) had to | used to have to | was having to | (she, he, it, one) had to | used to have to | was having to | (you) (sing formal)) had to | used to have to | were having to*
típico	*typical*
tipo (m)	*type, kind, sort*
tirar	*(to) throw, pull | throwing, pulling*
tomar el sol	*(to) sunbathe | sunbathing*
La Tomatina (f)	*Tomatina festival*
tortilla (f)	*omelette, corn pancake (LatAm)*
tradición (f)	*tradition*
tradicional	*traditional*
transporte (m)	*transport, transportation*
tren (m)	*train*
turismo (m)	*tourism*
turista (mf)	*tourist*
unas	*some (fpl)*
único	*unique, only*
vacaciones (fpl)	*holidays*
vacío	*empty*
valle (m)	*valley*
vaso (m)	*glass*
ventana (f)	*window*
viajar	*(to) travel | travelling*
viaje (m)	*trip, journey, travel*
viento (m)	*wind, windy*
visitar	*(to) visit | visiting*
vista (a) (f)	*view (over, of)*
volver	*(to) return | returning*
vuelo (m)	*flight*

Foundation translation revision

Spanish to English

1 Complete each English translation with the correct word from the box. There are more words than gaps.

day rent omelette equipment hobby sport team holidays sandwich buy player

1 El baloncesto es mi pasatiempo favorito. — *Basketball is my favourite ....*

2 Mañana voy a tomar un bocadillo grande. — *Tomorrow I am going to have a big ....*

3 Vamos a alquilar una casa en la playa. — *We are going to .... a house on the beach.*

4 El equipo de fútbol es muy bueno. — *The football .... is very good.*

When translating from Spanish to English, read the whole text to help you understand individual words. Remember that the word order will sometimes be different between Spanish and English.

2 Circle the errors in each English translation. Then write the correct English translation underneath.

1 Siempre encuentro aplicaciones nuevas. — *I sometimes find new apps.*

....

2 Es un espectáculo peligroso. — *It is a dangerous festival.*

....

3 Hay mucho viento en la costa. — *There is a lot of rain on the coast.*

....

4 Por la tarde el jugador ganó el partido. — *In the afternoon the team won the match.*

....

3 Underline the Spanish parts in this tangled text. Then rewrite the whole text in English.

Me llamo Natalia. I love bailar y to sing y soy jugadora de baloncesto. Nunca veo series because creo que they are aburridas. I prefer encontrar apps with vídeos de bailes. Hace una semana me quedé in a hotel which era muy caro and it was lejos del mar.

Think about the word order.

My name is ....

....

....

....

....

4 Translate these sentences into English on a separate sheet.

1 Prefiero dormir en el autobús.

2 A veces recibo noticias en mi móvil.

3 Somos aficionados a las canciones rápidas.

4 Me quedé en una habitación privada con una ventana grande.

5 Mis amigos quieren venir al estadio para ver al cantante famoso.

English to Spanish

1 Read the paragraph and number the boxes next to the Spanish phrases to put them in the correct order.

I don't share images with my contacts, but I like to send messages. At the weekends we often go to the park to do sports. Yesterday it rained a lot, but it did not snow. My mum is going to stay in a house near the beach. I think beaches are incredible as I love swimming.

una casa cerca de la playa ☐	a menudo vamos al parque ☐
los fines de semana ☐	porque me encanta la natación ☐
me gusta mandar mensajes ☐	mi madre se va a quedar en ☐
para hacer deportes ☐	pero no nevó ☐
ayer llovió mucho ☐	no comparto imágenes ☐
pienso que las playas son increíbles ☐	con mis contactos, pero ☐

2 Unjumble the Spanish words to translate the English sentences.

1 We are going to see the singer in the concert. — en concierto a cantante al Vamos ver el

....

2 Yesterday we rented equipment at the campsite. — alquilamos en camping Ayer equipo el

....

3 In the afternoon I have to clean my room. — tengo tarde habitación la mi que limpiar Por

....

4 On the first day we bought tickets to travel to the castle. — para compramos al primer El día castillo billetes viajar

....

3 Use the English sentences to help you complete the Spanish translations.

1 I would like to reserve a table for five people with sea views.

Quisiera reservar una mesa para ....

2 You can find the luggage in the room.

Se puede encontrar ....

3 If you like festivals you must go to Spain.

Si te gustan ....

4 I often meet friends on the way to the park.

A menudo me encuentro con ....

4 Translate these sentences into Spanish on a separate sheet.

1 I always go to the swimming pool.

2 The festival is quite expensive.

3 When it's windy, we don't go by boat.

4 If you like to travel, you have to visit the coast.

Make sure this adjective agrees with the noun 'festival'.

Remember that 'by' with modes of transport is translated as *en*, apart from 'by foot', which is *a pie*.

Higher translation revision

Spanish to English

1 Underline the errors in each English translation. Then write the correct English translation underneath.

1 El camping era muy seguro. — *The hotel was quite safe.*

....

2 Aunque el alojamiento estaba limpio, no era un destino popular. — *Although the accommodation wasn't clean, it was not an interesting destination.*

....

3 La pareja recorrió la ciudad y descubrió muchos lugares lindos. — *The friends travelled all over the town and discovered a few pretty places.*

....

4 Nos alojamos en un hotel amplio con ascensor. — *I'm staying in a small hotel without a lift.*

....

2 Read this Spanish paragraph and complete the partial translation below.

El festival de música en la ciudad es enorme. Hay conciertos de cantantes famosos, comida rica y actividades para todos. Es necesario comprar las entradas antes del evento. El ambiente es increíble y los fuegos artificiales por la noche son especiales.

The music .... in the city is .... There are .... of famous ...., delicious .... and activities for .... It's .... to buy .... before the event. The .... is incredible and the .... at night are special.

3 Use the Spanish sentences to help you complete the English translations.

1 A veces las personas con discapacidad encuentran problemas en el transporte público.

Sometimes disabled people ....

2 Alquilamos una casa, pero no tenía ni vasos ni tenedores.

We rented a house, but ....

3 Tampoco había piscina y la ventana estaba rota.

Neither was there a ....

4 Ayer el plato que probamos en el restaurante fue el mejor.

Yesterday the dish that ....

5 Cuando viajo en metro, el ruido me molesta mucho.

When I travel ....

4 Translate this paragraph into English on a separate sheet.

Siempre vamos al valle cerca de nuestra casa. Es hermoso con muchos árboles. La semana pasada descubrimos algunas costumbres culturales cuando fuimos a una fiesta allí. Había un desfile con mucha gente y fue increíble. Me gustaría volver el año que viene, pero con mi tarjeta porque la comida es cara.

English to Spanish

1 Unjumble the Spanish words to translate the English sentences.

1 Of course, during the holidays we appreciate the white sand.

la blanca las apreciamos Por durante en arena vacaciones la supuesto playa

2 We usually do sightseeing when we visit new places.

cuando turismo lugares hacer Solemos visitamos nuevos

3 The good thing is that you can take advantage of the good weather.

buen es puede aprovechar el bueno Lo que se clima

4 I almost never post photos on social media, although I often use electronic devices.

redes las menudo utilizo aparatos en cuelgo sociales nunca Casi fotos aunque a electrónicos

5 We watched a documentary about some music stars, but normally I prefer to watch comedies.

comedias normalmente ver sobre prefiero música de un Vimos estrellas documental algunas pero

2 Underline the English parts in this tangled text. Then rewrite the whole text in Spanish underneath.

Creo que Internet can be dangerous porque en many apps tenemos unknown followers. Social media también atraen many problems. People always se queja mucho. No tengo plans for this fin de semana, pero si mi amigo is free, we are going to go out a comer.

3 Translate this paragraph into Spanish on a separate sheet.

At the weekends we do lots of activities. I prefer to watch films at home. I think that going to the cinema is the worst thing as there is lots of noise. Last time the sound did not work. Next weekend we are going to travel to a hotel inside a natural park with a group of friends.

Use an expression with *lo*.

Translate this with two words.

Remember to check that your adjectives agree with the noun. It's a good idea to read over each sentence and check this carefully when you have finished each translation.

Zona de cultura ¡No hay dos familias iguales!

Using possessive adjectives

1 Draw lines to match up the Spanish words with their English translations.

1 la abuela	**a** mother
2 los padres	**b** sister
3 los primos	**c** grandmother
4 la hermana	**d** aunt
5 la tía	**e** stepbrother
6 la madre	**f** cousins
7 el hermanastro	**g** parents

2 Complete the sentences using the words in the box. There are more words than gaps.

abuelos	casa
ropa	hermano
hija	madres
niños	prima

1 Nuestras .... son muy trabajadoras.

2 Mis dos .... son mayores pero muy activos.

3 El coche de mi .... es viejo y de color negro.

4 Me gusta la .... de mi vecina. Es muy simpática.

5 Mi .... es la hija de mis tíos.

6 Los .... pequeños son muy agradables.

3 Rewrite each sentence, putting the words into the correct order.

1 bastante es grande familia Su

....

2 dos primo niños Mi tiene

....

3 tíos Barcelona Nuestros viven en

....

4 casa no padres tienen en Tus animales

....

5 muy hermanastra responsable es Vuestra

....

G

To show **possession**, you need to use a possessive adjective. Each one has a singular and plural form but ***nuestro*** and ***vuestro*** also have masculine and feminine forms.

	singular	**plural**
my	mi	mis
your (singular)	tu	tus
his/her/its	su	sus
our	nuestro/nuestra	nuestros/nuestras
your (plural)	vuestro/vuestra	vuestros/vuestras
their	su	sus

4 Translate these phrases into Spanish.

1 our family ....

2 his elder son ....

3 your (singular) boyfriend ....

4 their dog ....

5 your (plural) rabbit ....

6 my mum ....

H 7 her stepmother's house ....

H 8 our twin sons ....

H 9 my feelings ....

H 10 your (plural) grandparents' family traditions ....

H 5 Complete these sentences by translating the words in brackets.

1 El hijo de .... (*my cousins*) solo tiene cinco semanas: es un bebé.

2 .... (*her brother*) es .... (*my dad*).

3 .... (*your (singular) sister*) es lesbiana.

4 .... (*your (plural) uncle*) es una persona optimistc.

5 Dan un regalo y un pastel a .... (*their twin sons*) para celebrar .... (*their birthday*).

6 Mi marido y yo nos casamos hace dos años y vivimos en .... (*our own home*).

F 6 Translate these sentences into English.

1 Soy una persona feliz. ....

2 Mi hermana menor es muy seria. ....

3 Vivimos en una casa cerca del parque. ....

4 El sábado pasado jugué al fútbol con mi prima.

....

5 Me encanta reunirme con mis amigos los domingos.

....

H 7 Translate this paragraph into Spanish on a separate sheet.

Put the word for 'often' at the beginning of the sentence.

My stepmother and my father are very nice. We live in a multicultural town near the coast. I often look after my cousins on Saturdays. My aunt can count on me while she is working. Last week I went with my boyfriend to the beach on Saturday.

Use *conmigo* here.

1 Esta es mi gente

- Using the present continuous
- Using *ser* for physical descriptions and *estar* for location

1 Complete these sentences with the correct form of the verb *estar*.

1 Mi perro .... comiendo la carne.
2 Ellos .... comprando un billete de tren.
3 Nosotros .... bebiendo agua.
4 Yo .... yendo al cine con mi novia.
5 Vosotras .... nadando en la piscina.
6 Tú .... pidiendo algo para comer.

2 Circle the correct present participle to complete each sentence.

1 Estoy **bebiendo** / **escribiendo** una lista para ir de compras.
2 Mi tío está **trabajando** / **diciendo** en el jardín.
3 Nosotras estamos **bailando** / **jugando** a la videoconsola.
4 Estás **saliendo** / **durmiendo** en la cama.
5 Mis padres están **hablando** / **poniendo** con mi profesor.
6 Estáis **cocinando** / **leyendo** una buena paella.

G

Use the **present continuous tense** to say what someone is doing. Use the present tense of ***estar*** + **present participle**. To form the present participle, remove the ***-ar***, ***-er***, ***-ir*** from the <u>infinitive</u> and add the endings ***-ando*** (for ***-ar*** verbs) or ***-iendo*** (for ***-er*** and ***-ir*** verbs).

	estar (*to be*)	***present participle*** (*'ing' form*)
(yo)	estoy	bail**ando** com**iendo** sal**iendo**
(tú)	estás	
(él/ella/usted)	está	
(nosotros/as)	estamos	
(vosotros/as)	estáis	
(ellos/as/ustedes)	están	

Remember that there are some irregular present participles:

decir ⟶ ***diciendo***
dormir ⟶ ***durmiendo***
ir ⟶ ***yendo***
leer ⟶ ***leyendo***
pedir ⟶ ***pidiendo***

3 Circle the correct verb to complete each sentence.

1 Mi amigo Diego **es** / **está** muy alto.
2 Nosotros **estamos** / **somos** rubios.
3 Yo **estoy** / **soy** bastante baja.
4 Mi casa **es** / **está** cerca de la plaza.
5 Los profesores **son** / **están** en el patio.
6 ¿Dónde **eres** / **estás**, Fátima?
H 7 Vosotras **sois** / **estáis** irritantes.
H 8 Los mayores **son** / **están** en casa hoy.

G

The verbs ***ser*** and ***estar*** both mean 'to be' in English.
Use the verb ***estar*** when talking about location or state.
Use the verb ***ser*** when talking about physical description.

	estar (*to be*)	**ser** (*to be*)
(yo)	estoy	soy
(tú)	estás	eres
(él/ella/usted)	está	es
(nosotros/as)	estamos	somos
(vosotros/as)	estáis	sois
(ellos/ellas/ustedes)	están	son

4 Álex is describing a photo of herself, her family and a friend. Complete the paragraph using the words in the box. There are more words than gaps.

En la foto hay cuatro personas. Yo estoy en el primer plano con mi .... amigo Juan. Mis padres están en el .... plano. Soy bastante .... Tengo los ojos .... Soy como mi .... porque las dos tenemos el pelo .... y castaño. A veces llevo ...., por ejemplo, cuando quiero leer en clase. Mi amigo Juan es pelirrojo y tiene la .... muy pequeña y el pelo corto.

H Juan tiene tres hermanos y es el .... de todos. Nunca está .... y es un amigo muy fiel. Nos juntamos a .... los fines de semana. Al .... de la foto está nuestro jardín.

alta	madre
enfadado	gafas
fondo	hermano
largo	corta
marrones	nariz
mejor	segundo
mayor	menudo
bajo	pantalones

H 5 Complete these sentences by translating the words in brackets.

1 .... (*They (m) are*) separando la ropa.

2 Estoy .... (*reading the content*) del blog.

3 .... (*You (singular) are*) discutiendo con tu padre.

4 .... (*We (f) are*) caminando por el campo.

5 Estáis .... (*explaining the advantages*) del proyecto.

6 .... (*The boys are*) escuchando a su profesora.

F 6 Translate these sentences into Spanish.

1 I have blue eyes. ....

2 I am taller than my girlfriend. ....

3 She is reading a message on her phone. ....

4 We listened to music in my room yesterday. ....

The phrase 'than I am' translates simply as *que yo*.

5 My younger brother is more like my father than I am.

....

H 7 Translate this paragraph into English.

Mi hermana es adoptada. No se parece a nosotros porque es morena con ojos marrones. Hacemos muchas cosas juntas porque nos llevamos bien y confío en ella. Somos bastante similares y ¡tenemos la misma fecha de nacimiento! Hace dos días fuimos al cine para ver una película y nos encantó. ¡La última parte fue muy original!

....

....

....

....

2 ¿A quién sigues?

Using the personal *a* • Using the 'he/she/it' form of the preterite tense

1 Add the personal *a* to these sentences if it is needed.

1 Veo .... muchos vídeos de música en Internet.
2 Invité .... mi amigo a un museo de moda.
3 Sigo .... muchos artistas que me gustan.
4 Escucho .... cantantes de música latina.
5 Leo .... un blog sobre cocina cada día.
6 Veo .... personas interesantes en las redes.

G

We use the **personal *a*** when the object of the verb is a person.
*Sigo **a** muchas personas famosas.*
I follow many famous people.

Do **not** use it if the object is **not** a person.
Sigo canales de música.
I follow music channels.

2 Circle the correct form of the verb to complete each sentence.

1 **Me interesa** / **me interesan** mucho la cocina española.
2 **No me importa** / **no me importan** seguir a personas famosas.
3 **Me importa** / **me importan** mucho los deportes.
4 **Me interesa** / **me interesan** buscar a nuevos amigos en la red.
5 **No me interesa** / **no me interesan** los datos falsos porque son inútiles.
6 **Me importa** / **me importan** mis padres y mi familia.

G

Impersonal verbs like ***interesar*** and ***importar*** work like ***gustar*** and ***encantar***.
With a verb or singular noun, use **me interesa** or **me importa**.

Me interesa el fútbol.	I am interested in football.
Me importa sacar buenas notas.	Getting good grades is important to me.

With a plural noun, use ***me interesan*** or ***me importan***.

Me interesan los juegos de la videoconsola.	I am interested in video console games.
Me importan mis amigos.	My friends are important to me.

3 Draw lines to match up the Spanish verbs with their English translations.

1 fue	a he/she did
2 mandó	b he/she caught the train
3 habló	c he/she explained
4 escuchó	d he/she was
5 hizo	e he/she was born
6 tomó el sol	f he/she sent
7 cogió el tren	g he/she sunbathed
8 describió	h he/she spoke
H 9 nació	i he/she described
H 10 explicó	j he/she listened

G

Use the **preterite tense** to talk about completed actions in the past. To talk about someone else (he/she), for **-*ar*** verbs, use the ending **-*ó***. The accent is very important to show that we are talking about the past.
*Mi hermana **bailó** en el colegio ayer.*
*Mi amigo **compró** un regalo.*

For **-*er*/-*ir*** verbs, use the ending **-*ió***.
*El niño **salió** a la calle.*
*El perro **comió** el pan.*

Remember that some verbs have their own pattern:
ser → ***fue*** (he/she was)
tener → ***tuvo*** (he/she had)
hacer → ***hizo*** (he/she did)

4 Complete the sentences using the verbs from the box. There are more words than gaps.

comió	creó	entró
abrió	salió	cerró
luchó	terminó	tuvo
bebió	organizó	preguntó

1 Marcos .... mucha agua ayer.

2 Mi hermana .... sus deberes por la tarde.

3 Sara .... una fiesta de cumpleaños para su madre.

4 El niño .... sueño.

H 5 El artista .... mucha belleza en su arte.

H 6 Lola .... por los derechos de las personas transgénero.

H 5 Complete the sentences by changing the verb in brackets into the he/she/it form of the preterite. Then translate them into English.

1 El abuelo .... al niño. (*abrazar*)

....

2 El hombre se .... en el jardín ayer. (*relajar*)

Relajarse is a reflexive verb. Here the reflexive pronoun is already in the sentence.

....

3 La mamá .... a su hijo a la escuela. (*acompañar*) ....

4 Nuestro tío .... en Latinoamérica. (*crecer*) ....

5 Paula .... la casa por la mañana. (*limpiar*) ....

6 Tu amigo .... su dinero contigo. (*compartir*) ....

F 6 Translate these sentences into English.

1 Escucho a muchos cantantes. ....

2 Me interesa ver vídeos de música. ....

3 A veces sigo canales de moda. ....

4 Me encanta mi modelo de conducta porque es guay. ....

....

5 El año pasado ella ayudó a muchos niños pobres. ....

....

H 7 Translate this paragraph into Spanish.

I have been following a European singer for a year. She has a positive personality and hates discrimination. She identifies as bisexual and wants equality for everyone. Last month, she criticised some people on social media. I think that she supports women and encourages them to fight for more representation in society.

....

....

....

....

....

3 ¡Amigos para siempre!

- Using reflexive verbs • Choosing which tense to use
- H Using the pronouns *me* and *te* before a verb

1 Draw lines to match up the sentence halves.

1 Me llevo bien
2 Pasamos
3 Tengo mucho
4 Hago muchas
5 Es muy responsable
6 Nunca

a y divertido.
b en común con él.
c con mi amigo Diego.
d discutimos.
e cosas con él.
f mucho tiempo juntos.

G

Some verbs for describing relationships are **reflexive** in Spanish. Watch out for those that are also stem-changing in the present tense, such as ***divertirse*** and ***reírse***.

	llevarse (*to get on*)	**divertirse** (*to have fun*)	**reírse** (*to laugh*)
(yo)	**me** llevo	**me** div**ie**rto	me r**í**o
(tú)	**te** llevas	**te** div**ie**rtes	te r**íe**s
(él/ella/usted)	**se** lleva	**se** div**ie**rte	se r**íe**

2 Add the correct reflexive pronoun (*me, te, se*) in front of each verb.

1 Mi mejor amigo .... llama Hugo.
2 ¿Tú .... ríes cuando estás jugando a la videoconsola?
3 Mi padrastro .... lleva muy bien con nosotros.
4 .... divierto cuando veo vídeos en las redes.
5 Tú .... llevas muy bien con tu hermano.
6 .... río con mis amigas.

3 Ana has written a blog about friendship. Fill in the gaps by using a verb from the box below.

juntamos
tenemos
estamos
río
discutimos
divierto
hacemos
paso
son
gustan

Mis amigos son muy importantes en mi vida. .... mucho tiempo con ellos y me .... Siempre .... juntos y no .... nunca. .... mucho en común, como la música, la moda y la videoconsola. Nos .... las mismas cosas. Me .... con ellos y .... muchas actividades.

H Mis amigos .... positivos y fieles. Nos .... todos los fines de semana.

G

Remember that time phrases may help you identify the verb **tense**.
Preterite: *ayer, la semana pasada, el mes pasado, el año pasado*
Present: *hoy, ahora, en este momento, todos los días*
Future: *mañana, la semana próxima, el mes próximo, el año próximo*

4 Circle the correct time phrase to complete the sentences.

1 **Ayer / En este momento** fui al cine con mi novia.

2 **Mañana / La semana pasada** mi amigo va a buscar vídeos en Internet.

3 Me encanta mirar las redes sociales **el mes pasado / todos los días**.

4 **Ahora / Mañana** me llevo bien con mi familia.

5 Mi padre me ayudó mucho **ahora / el año pasado**.

H 6 El profesor tiene que darle un consejo al niño **ayer / esta tarde**.

H 7 Compré ropa nueva **el año próximo / el mes pasado** y ¡me costó un ojo de la cara!

The word *cara* means 'face' in this sentence but this is an idiomatic expression that means 'it cost me an arm and a leg'.

When using the pronouns ***me*** and ***te***, remember to put them in front of the verb. **G**

H **5 Underline the English parts in these sentences. Then rewrite them in Spanish.**

1 Mi amigo guarda lo que le digo para sí mismo y *helps me*. ....

2 ¿Quién *supports you* más, tus amigos o tu familia? ....

3 La amistad *is important to me*. ....

4 Un buen amigo es alguien que *accepts you* como eres. ....

5 Mi abuela siempre *gives me* muchos besos. ....

6 Tú siempre *tell me* la verdad. ....

F **6 Translate these sentences into Spanish.**

1 My best friend is cheerful. ....

2 We have a lot in common and I laugh with him. ....

3 We are always together at weekends. ....

4 Last Saturday, we watched a film at my house. ....

5 It is important to listen and respect other people. ....

....

H **7 Translate this paragraph into English.**

Me llevo muy bien con la gente de mi clase. Nunca nos peleamos y puedo contar totalmente con ellos. Mi mejor amiga me apoya en todo y nunca me juzga. Es una persona de confianza para mí porque siempre me acepta como soy. La semana pasada fuimos a una fiesta donde nos divertimos mucho.

....

....

....

....

4 Así soy yo

Using direct object pronouns • Using *para* + infinitive

1 Draw lines to match up the Spanish phrases with their English translations.

1 Creo que	**a** I want
2 Mi sueño es	**b** It matters to me
3 En mi opinión	**c** I think that
4 Quiero	**d** For me
5 Para mí	**e** My dream is
6 Me importa	**f** In my opinion

2 Read what Cris says about themselves. Complete the text by filling each gap with a word from the box.

Soy Cris. Este es mi blog. Pienso que soy bastante .... y muy social. Para mí, la identidad es .... Soy transgénero y mi familia me .... mucho. Hay mucho .... entre nosotros y tenemos una relación fuerte. Me .... vivir en una .... donde hay mucho amor.

> responsable
> ama cariño
> importante
> sociedad
> encanta

G

A **direct object pronoun** replaces the noun which has just been mentioned, like 'him/her/it/them' in English. It helps to avoid repetition. Remember to pay attention to grammatical agreement.

	masculine	**feminine**
singular	***lo*** (him/it)	***la*** (her/it)
plural	***los*** (them)	***las*** (them)

The pronoun usually goes before the conjugated verb:
Veo vídeos divertidos. ***Los*** *veo en las redes sociales.*

3 Complete the sentences by adding the correct direct object pronoun (*lo*/*la*/*los*/*las*).

1 Sigo a una cantante joven. .... escucho mucho.

2 Mi padre tiene un coche nuevo. .... compró en julio.

3 Creo que Internet es muy útil. .... uso para mis deberes.

4 Me encantan los vídeos de música. .... veo todos los días.

5 Las redes sociales son importantes para la comunicación. .... uso mucho.

> Remember that *fotos* is feminine. The full word is *fotografías*.

6 A menudo quiero mandar fotos a mis amigos. .... comparto en Internet.

H **7** Mi hermano gemelo perdió su bolsa. .... va a buscar en casa.

H **8** Las críticas son bastante malas, pero el actor .... respeta.

4 Complete these sentences by translating the words in brackets.

1 Veo vídeos .... (*in order to listen to*) música.

2 Nadim usa las redes sociales .... (*for chatting*) con sus amigos.

3 Sigo canales de dibujo .... (*in order to learn*) más sobre el arte.

4 Tengo que hacer más ....(*to protect*) el planeta.

5 Sofía hace la compra a la gente mayor de su barrio .... (*to help*) a su comunidad.

6 Uso esta aplicación en mi móvil .... (*for sending*) mensajes.

H 7 Tienes que escuchar .... (*in order to understand*) el problema.

H 8 Los jóvenes se presentan en canales de vídeo .... (*in order to express themselves*).

G

Use ***para*** to mean '**in order to**' or '**for ...-ing**'. It must be followed by an infinitive if you are using a verb.
Uso las redes sociales ***para*** *compartir fotos con mis amigos.*
I use social networks **for** sharing photos with my friends.

H **5 Draw lines to match up the two halves of the sentences about giving opinions and information.**

1 Creo que pasar horas en las redes sociales	a todos los países del mundo.
2 Me preocupan mucho	b y es optimista para el futuro.
3 Mi sueño es ver la paz en	c es una pérdida de tiempo.
4 Mi amigo se identifica como no binario	d y tengo el deseo de aprender más.
5 En mi opinión, los padres tienen que	e los animales en peligro.
6 Me interesan mis derechos	f limitar las horas en la videoconsola.

F **6 Translate these sentences into English.**

1 Pienso que soy muy social. ....

2 La educación es importante para mí. ....

3 También me importa la cultura de mi país. ....

4 Ayer leí un blog interesante sobre la naturaleza. ....

5 Mi sueño es proteger a todos los animales en peligro. ....

....

H **7 Translate this paragraph into Spanish.**

I am hard-working and optimistic. I believe that technology can be useful, but there are disadvantages. Last week I used social media to send messages to my friends. I worry a lot about animal rights and justice in the world. My aim is to do something to help protect the planet in the future.

....

....

....

....

5 Necesito ayuda, ¿qué puedo hacer?

- Using *estar* to express moods
- Using *querer/poder* + infinitive or H *podrías/deberías* + infinitive

1 Complete the sentences with the correct form of *estar*.

1 Mi hermano mayor .... muy solo.

2 Yo nunca .... triste.

3 ¿Cómo .... tú?

4 Creo que mi amiga .... enfadada.

5 Tú .... contento hoy.

6 Yo .... cansada hoy porque trabajé mucho ayer.

> **G** Use the verb ***estar*** to describe **feelings, emotions** and **mood.**
> ***Estoy*** *contento/a*
> ***Estoy*** *triste*
> ***Está*** *enfadado/a*
> ***Está*** *cansado/a*

2 Use *nunca, nada* or *nadie* to make these sentences negative. Think about the position of the negative word in Spanish.

1 La niña (*never*) juega al fútbol. ....

2 Yo compré (*nothing*) ayer. ....

3 No quiero ver a (*nobody*). ....

4 (*Never*) tengo tiempo para ver la tele. ....

5 Hay (*nothing*) interesante en este blog. ....

> **G** Using negatives like ***nunca*** (never), ***nada*** (nothing) and ***nadie*** (nobody / no one) can be done in two ways. You can put the negative word before the verb.
>
> | | |
> |---|---|
> | ***Nunca*** *voy a la costa.* | I **never** go to the coast. |
> | ***Nada*** *pasó ayer.* | **Nothing** happened yesterday. |
> | ***Nadie*** *quiere venir.* | **Nobody** wants to go. |
>
> Alternatively, the verb can be sandwiched between ***no*** and the negative word.
>
> ***No*** *voy* ***nunca*** *a la costa.*   ***No*** *pasó* ***nada*** *ayer.*   ***No*** *quiere venir* ***nadie***.

3 Draw lines to match up the problems with the advice.

1 Mi mejor amigo está enfadado y no sé por qué.

2 Tengo problemas con mis deberes.

3 Mi hermanastra no se lleva bien con su mejor amiga y está sola.

4 No tengo mucho dinero y quiero comprar un regalo para mi novia.

5 Mi madre siempre está triste y nunca sonríe.

6 Mi abuelo está enfermo y no puede salir con su perro.

a Debes pasar tiempo con ella y hacer actividades juntas.

b Tienes que pasear al perro por él.

c Debes sentarte con ella para preguntar cómo la puedes ayudar.

d Tienes que hablar con él para ver cuál es el problema.

e Puedes pedir ayuda a la profesora.

f Puedes encontrar un trabajo para los sábados.

> **G** Use ***tienes que***, ***debes*** and ***puedes*** followed by the <u>infinitive</u> to give advice or suggestions.
>
> ***Poder*** (to be able to / can) and ***querer*** (to want) are both stem-changing verbs. If they are followed by another verb, the second verb must be in the <u>infinitive</u>.

4 Complete these sentences with the correct form of the verbs *poder* or *querer*.

1 El niño no .... leer las letras de la página porque no tiene sus gafas. (*poder*)

2 Yo no .... ir al concierto; no me interesa ese género de música religiosa. (*querer*)

3 ¿Tú me .... describir tu conversación con el director? (*poder*)

4 Tú nunca .... estar con tu familia cercana. (*querer*)

H 5 Los adultos no .... tener conflictos con las otras generaciones. (*querer*)

H 6 Jalil es una persona auténtica; nosotros .... confiar en él. (*poder*)

H 7 El uso sin control de las redes sociales .... causar problemas entre los jóvenes. (*poder*)

H You can offer advice by using the conditional form of ***deber*** and ***poder***. **G**
deberías (you should) ***podrías*** (you could)

H 5 Read each problem and rewrite these sentences to give the correct advice.

1 Me identifico como gay, pero mis primos son heterosexuales y no entienden mis problemas.

ellos tener cómo discusión con para una explicar te Deberías sientes

....

2 No me relaciono con otras personas e ignoro por qué. Me siento solo.

actividades Podrías en con más algunas frecuencia participar

....

3 Me siento triste y enfadado, y no tengo mucho orgullo.

sentimientos tus Deberías tu compartir con familia ....

4 Por lo general, no duermo bien. Me siento muy cansado en el colegio.

con el Podrías un médico hablar ....

5 No tengo mucha fe en el futuro del planeta y esto me pone nerviosa.

expertos Deberías consejos de leer los los ....

F 6 Translate these sentences into Spanish.

1 I am lonely and I want to make friends. ....

2 If you are never happy when you go to school, you must talk to your teacher.

....

3 My parents are kind and they love me a lot. ....

4 Yesterday, I did an activity in order to meet international people.

....

H 7 Translate this paragraph into English on a separate sheet.

Desde hace un año me siento diferente. Nunca me relaciono bien con otras personas en el colegio. No salgo a comer fuera con nadie los fines de semana. Mi madre dice que debería aprender a tocar un instrumento musical. Pienso que la presión del grupo es negativa y significa que hay mucha discriminación.

Glossary

bold = this word will appear in Higher exams only

abrazar	*(to) hug | hugging*			
abuela (f)	*grandmother*			
abuelo (m)	*grandfather, grandparent*			
acompañar	*(to) accompany, go with*			
adulto (m), adulta (f)	*adult*			
alguien	*someone*			
alto	*tall, high, loud*			
amar	*(to) love | loving*			
amistad (f)	*friendship*			
amor (m)	*love*			
animal (m)	*animal*			
-astro, -astra, -astros, -astras	*step-*			
auténtico	*authentic*			
azul	*blue*			
bajo	*short, low*			
bebé (mf)	*baby*			
belleza (f)	*beauty*			
beso (m)	*kiss*			
bien	*well, good*			
bisexual	*bisexual*			
blog (m)	*blog*			
buscar	*(to) look for, search | looking for, searching*			
canal (m)	*channel, canal*			
cara (f)	*face*			
cariño (m)	*affection, love*			
casarse	*(to) get married | getting married*			
castaño	*chestnut brown*			
cercano	*close, closely-related, nearby*			
cocinar	*(to) cook | cooking*			
color (m)	*colour*			
común	*common*			
comunicación (f)	*communication*			
conejo (m)	*rabbit*			
confianza (f)	*confidence, trust*			
confiar en	*(to) rely on*			
conflicto (m)	*conflict*			
conmigo	*with me*			
consejo (m)	*advice*			
contar; contar con	*(to) count, tell; (to) count on*			
contenido (m)	*content*			
contento	*happy, content*			
contigo	*with you (sing informal)*			
control (m)	*control, test*			
conversación (f)	*conversation*			
corto	*short, brief*			
cosa (f)	*thing*			
crear	*(to) create*			
crítica (f)	*review, criticism*			
criticar	*(to) criticise*			
cuidar (de)	*(to) look after*			
cumpleaños (m)	*birthday*			
dar	*(to) give | giving*			
datos (mpl)	*data*			
describir	*(to) describe | describing*			
deseo (m)	*desire, wish*			
desde hace (+ present tense)	*to have been + -ing + for + time*			
desventaja (f)	*disadvantage, con*			
diferente	*different*			
discriminación (f)	*discrimination*			

discusión (f)	*discussion, argument*
discutir	*(to) argue, discuss | arguing, discussing*
divertirse	*(to) enjoy oneself | enjoying oneself*
dormir; dormirse	*(to) sleep, fall asleep | sleeping, falling asleep*
educación (f)	*education*
el mayor, la mayor, los mayores, las mayores	*the oldest*
enfadado	*angry*
entender	*(to) understand*
eres	*(you (sing informal)) are*
esto	*this (n)*
europeo	*European*
experto (m), experta (f)	*expert*
explicar	*(to) explain*
expresar(se)	*(to) express (oneself)*
falso	*false*
familia (f)	*family*
fe (f)	*faith*
feliz	*happy*
fiel	*loyal, faithful*
fondo (m)	*background, bottom*
frecuencia (f)	*frequency*
fuera; fuera de	*out, outside, away; outside of, away from*
fuerte	*strong*
gafas (fpl)	*glasses*
gay	*gay*
gemelo	*twin*

generación (f)	*generation*
general	*general*
género (m)	*gender, genre*
guardar	*(to) keep, store, save*
guay	*cool*
hermana (f)	*sister*
hermano (m)	*brother, sibling*
heterosexual	*straight*
hija (f)	*daughter, child*
hijo (m)	*son, child*
hogar (m)	*home*
hombre (m)	*man*
identidad (f)	*identity*
identificarse (con)	*(to) identify (with)*
ignorar	*(to) ignore, not know*
igualdad (f)	*equality*
importante	*important*
importar	*(to) matter | mattering*
instrumento (m)	*instrument*
internacional	*international*
inútil	*useless*
invitar	*(to) invite | inviting*
irritante	*annoying*
joven	*young*
juego (m)	*game*
juntarse	*(to) meet, get together*
juntos	*together*
juzgar	*(to) judge*
le	*him (m) (obj) | (to) him, (to) her, (to) it (indirect obj)*
lesbiana	*lesbian*

letra (f)	*letter, lyrics*
leyendo	*reading*
limitar	*(to) limit*
lista (f)	*list*
llamar; llamarse	*(to) call, phone / calling, phoning; (to) be called / being called*
los mayores (mpl)	*adults, the elderly*
madre (f)	*mother*
mamá (f)	*mum*
marido (m)	*husband*
marrón	*brown*
mayor	*elder, eldest, larger, main*
menor	*younger, youngest*
mientras	*while, whereas*
mismo	*same*
moda (f); a la moda, de moda	*fashion; fashionable*
modelo de conducta	*role model*
moreno	*dark (hair), tanned (skin)*
multicultural	*multicultural*
musical	*musical*
nacer	*(to) be born / being born*
nacimiento (m)	*birth*
nadie, (no) nadie	*nobody, no one, anybody (after negative verb), anyone (after negative verb)*
nariz (f)	*nose*
negativo	*negative*
negro	*black*
niña (f)	*child, (young) girl*
no binario	*non-binary*
novia (f)	*girlfriend*
novio (m)	*boyfriend*
ojos (mpl)	*eyes*
opinión (f)	*opinion*
optimista	*optimistic*
organizar	*(to) organise / organising*
orgullo (m)	*pride*
original	*original*
padre (m)	*father, parent*
página (f)	*page*
papá (m)	*dad*
parte (f)	*part*
paz (f)	*peace*
pelearse	*(to) fight, argue*
pelirrojo	*red-haired, ginger*
pelo (m)	*hair*
pérdida (f)	*loss, waste*
perro (m)	*dog*
personalidad (f)	*personality*
presentar; presentarse	*(to) present, introduce (someone); (to) introduce oneself*
presión (f)	*pressure*
primer plano (m)	*foreground*
primo (m), prima (f)	*cousin*
problema (m)	*problem*
red (f)	*network, net*
relación (f)	*relationship, relation*
relacionar; relacionarse (con)	*(to) relate; to relate (to), interact (with)*
relajarse	*(to) relax*
religioso	*religious*

representación (f)	*representation*
respetar	*(to) respect | respecting*
responsable	*responsible*
reunirse	*(to) gather, meet | gathering, meeting*
rubio	*blonde, light (skin)*
sé	*(I) know (how to)*
segundo plano (m)	*background*
sentar(se)	*(to) sit down | sitting down*
sentimiento (m)	*feeling*
separar(se)	*(to) separate, sort, split up*
ser	*(to) be | being*
significar	*(to) mean | meaning*
similar	*similar*
social	*social*
somos	*(we) are | have been*
sonreír	*(to) smile | smiling*
tengo; tengo que	*(I) have | am having; have to, must | am having to*
tía (f)	*aunt*
tiene; tiene que	*(she, he, it, one) has | is having | (you (sing formal)) have | (she, he, it, one) has to, must | is having to | (you (sing formal)) have to, must | are having to*
tienen; tienen que	*(they) have | are having | (you (pl formal)) have | are having; (they) have to, must | are having to | (you (pl formal)) have to, must | are having to*
tienes; tienes que	*(you (sing informal)) have |* ***are having****; have to, must | are having to*
tío (m)	*uncle*
totalmente	*totally, completely*
transgénero	*transgender*
triste	*sad, unhappy*
útil	*useful*
ventaja (f)	*advantage, pro*
vida (f)	*life*
vivir	*(to) live | living*
vuestro, vuestra, vuestros, vuestras	*your (pl informal) (m, f, mpl, fpl)*

Zona de cultura ¡Qué rico!

Using adjectives of nationality

1 Draw lines to match up the sentence halves according to the time shown on each clock.

1 Tomo el desayuno a

2 Mi madre siempre bebe un café a

3 Me gusta comer un bocadillo a

4 Tomo el almuerzo a

5 Me gusta descansar un poco a

6 Tomo la cena con mi familia a

a las diez y media de la mañana.

b las nueve y media de la noche.

c las dos y cuarto de la tarde.

d las ocho y media de la mañana.

e mediodía.

f las cinco de la tarde.

Use ***a las*** + **number** to talk about time in Spanish: *voy al colegio* ***a las ocho***.
Add ***de la mañana/tarde/noche*** to make the time of the day clear: *a las ocho* ***de la tarde***.
Add ***y media*** to talk about half past the hour: *a las ocho* ***y media***.
Add ***y cuarto*** to talk about quarter past the hour: *a las ocho* ***y cuarto***.

2 Circle the correct adjective of nationality to complete each sentence.

1 Carla es **mexicanos / mexicana**, pero ahora vive en Barcelona.

2 Indra y Miguel son de Latinoamérica. Son **chilenos / chilena**.

3 Mi tía es **inglés / inglesa**, pero ahora vive en las Islas Baleares.

4 El amigo de mi madre es **peruana / peruano**.

5 Mi abuela y mi abuelo son de Medellín. Son **colombianas / colombianos**.

6 Mi profesora es de Buenos Aires. Es **argentino / argentina**.

3 Read what people say about food and complete each sentence using a word from the box. There are more words than gaps.

bocadillo	restaurante
pasta	arroz
restaurante	azúcar
compras	vegana
dieta	leche
sed	merienda
almuerzo	tapas

1 Para el desayuno, tomo pan y un café con ....

2 Me gusta mucho la .... Mi madre la prepara para la cena.

3 Mi hermana dice que me va a preparar una comida ....

4 Siempre como arroz con pescado para el ....

5 Mi padre toma la .... a las cuatro exactamente. Siempre toma té con un pastel.

6 A veces mi novio toma churros con chocolate. Son ricos, pero tienen mucho ....

H 7 La paella consiste en .... con carne o pescado y verduras.

H 8 Diría que tengo una .... equilibrada.

4 Rewrite each sentence, putting the words into the correct order.

1 me mucho La cubana gusta comida. ....

2 estoy siesta porque muy a la Voy pronto cansada dormir. ....

3 el fruta amiga para compró mucha postre Mi. ....

4 preparó queso cena Mi una huevos buena con y padre. ....

H 5 de hay mi No suficiente colegio en comida la variedad. ....

H 6 hace cocina Tu año un hermano probó la vegetariana. ....

H **5 Read the conversation between Amira and Toni about Toni's recent visit to her aunt's house. Match Toni's answers to Amira's questions by putting the letters in the correct boxes.**

Amira

1 Hola, ¿cómo estás? ¿Cómo fue tu visita a tu tía en verano? ☐

2 ¿Por qué? ☐

3 Entiendo lo que dices. Pero tu tía vive cerca de la costa, ¿no? ¿No fuiste a la playa? ☐

4 Claro. ¿Cómo te sientes ahora? ☐

5 Entonces, ¿vas a visitar a tu tía otra vez a pesar de la comida? ☐

6 Pero no tienes amigos allí... ☐

Toni

a Diría que sí. Voy a enseñarle cómo hacer platos más ricos.

b Mejor, gracias. La próxima vez voy a tener más cuidado.

c Conocí a una chica muy simpática en el hospital. Quiero volver a verla.

d La comida que cocina mi tía es simple y me parece un poco aburrida. Además, mi tía es bastante mayor ahora, vive en un pueblo tranquilo y no hay mucho que hacer.

e Claro que sí. La playa allí es muy bonita pero las instalaciones son viejas. Un día fui a correr y tuve un accidente: me caí y me hice daño en el brazo. Tuve que ir al hospital.

f Pues, lo pasé bien, pero no me gustó mucho la comida.

F **6 Translate these sentences into English on a separate sheet.**

1 Me gustan los entrantes españoles.

2 Tomo un desayuno ligero a las ocho.

3 Creo que las patatas fritas no son sanas.

4 Ayer a mediodía comí un bocadillo y bebí agua.

5 Es importante tener una buena dieta y también hacer ejercicio.

H **7 Translate this paragraph into Spanish on a separate sheet.**

It is interesting to eat in other countries. My sister tries to avoid everything that is unhealthy. When I went to the Canary Islands, I tried everything. I eat fresh meals, but I do not like the smell of fish. I want to learn to cook sweet things but without a lot of sugar.

1 ¿Llevas una vida sana?

Using indefinite adjectives • Using *tener* + noun

1 Draw lines to match up the sentence halves.

1 Me despierto muy temprano,
2 Después, me lavo
3 Me visto y tomo
4 Me preparo y luego
5 A las ocho voy

a en el cuarto de baño.
b al colegio a pie.
c el desayuno.
d a las seis.
e salgo de casa.

G

To talk about your daily routine, you will need to use some verbs that are **reflexive**.

	levantarse (to get up)
(yo) (tú) (él/ella/usted)	**me** levanto **te** levantas **se** levanta

Remember that some reflexive verbs are also stem-changing.
vestirse (to get dressed) → ***me vi̲sto***
despertarse (to wake up) → ***me despi̲e̲rto***

2 Complete the sentences below using the times given in brackets. Remember to add *de la mañana, de la tarde* or *de la noche* to the times when you need to make it clear.

Example: Paula se despierta a las seis y media de la mañana.

1 (7 a.m.) Paula se levanta ....
2 (7.30 a.m.) Se lava y se pone la ropa ....
3 (8 a.m.) Sale de casa ....
4 (1 p.m.) Toma el almuerzo ....
5 (5.30 p.m.) Vuelve del colegio ....
6 (10 p.m.) Se va a la cama ....

3 Draw lines to match up the Spanish phrases with their English meanings.

1 ¿Tienes sed?
2 Tiene razón.
3 Tengo mucho calor.
4 Tiene sueño.
5 ¿Tienes frío?
6 Tengo mucha hambre.

a He/She is sleepy.
b Are you cold?
c Are you thirsty?
d I am very hungry.
e He/She is right.
f I am very hot.

G

The verb **tener** (to have) is sometimes used with a noun in Spanish where the verb 'to be' is used in English.

Tengo *hambre.* I'm hungry.
Tengo *sed.* I'm thirsty.
Tengo *calor.* I'm hot.
Tengo *frío.* I'm cold.

4 Complete these sentences by translating the words in brackets.

1 Hay .... (*a lot of people*) en el parque hoy.

2 Creo que tengo .... (*too much homework*) esta noche.

3 .... (*Some days*) no oigo al profesor.

4 No todos tenemos los .... (*same problems*).

H 5 Quiero hacer .... (*other activities*) después de la práctica de fútbol.

H 6 Me acuesto .... (*every night*) a las diez.

H 7 .... (*Some weekends*) camino con mi hermana al gimnasio.

Remember that *problema* is a masculine word!

G Remember that indefinite adjectives like ***alguno*** and ***mismo*** agree in gender and number with the noun they are describing, and they come before the noun. The exception is ***cada*** (each/every), which is invariable.

H 5 **Rewrite these sentences using *antes de* or *después de* on a separate sheet. There are two possibilities for each one. The first sentence has been done as an example.**

1 Escribo algo en una hoja de papel. Me acuesto. Después de escribir algo en una hoja de papel, me acuesto. or Antes de acostarme, escribo algo en una hoja de papel.

2 Vuelves a casa a las cinco. Tomas la merienda en la cocina.

3 Carmen toma el desayuno. Se prepara para ir al colegio.

4 Me despierto a las siete. Me levanto.

5 Lin se lava en el cuarto de baño. Se viste en su habitación.

6 Preparo las verduras. Empiezo a cocinar.

G Use the expressions ***antes de*** and ***después de*** to talk about 'before' and 'after'.

If the next word is a noun, remember to use **de** + **article**: *después **del** almuerzo, después **de la** cena.*

H If the next word is a verb, it must be in the infinitive: *antes de llegar, después de comer*.

If the verb is reflexive, you need to add the correct reflexive pronoun to the infinitive: *antes de vestir**me**, después de despertar**se***.

F 6 **Translate these sentences into Spanish.**

1 I get up at 8 o'clock. ....

2 I wash myself and put on my clothes. ....

3 My sister always has the same things for breakfast before school.

....

4 Yesterday I ate a sandwich at midday in the park. ....

5 I like to do my homework before the afternoon snack.

....

H 7 **Translate this paragraph into English on a separate sheet.**

Nos levantamos bastante temprano. Mi hermano ayuda a mi madre antes de salir de casa. Yo pongo los cuchillos, las cucharas y los tenedores en la mesa. Algunos días voy al colegio a pie, pero el viernes pasado cogí el autobús. Es una buena idea moverte a pie, especialmente si quieres oír los pájaros por el camino.

2 ¿Somos lo que comemos?

Using *se necesita* and *hay que* + infinitive • Using direct object pronouns

1 Iván is talking about mealtimes in his country. Draw lines to match up the questions with the answers.

1 ¿Qué tomas parc el desayuno?	**a** Entre las ocho y las nueve de la noche.
2 ¿A qué hora tomas el almuerzo?	**b** Sí, tomo la merienda, un té con una fruta.
3 ¿Tomas algo al final de la tarde?	**c** Tomo pan con queso y café con leche.
4 ¿Dónde tomas la cena?	**d** Lo tomo a las dos normalmente.
5 ¿A qué hora?	**e** La tomo en casa con mis padres.

2 Replace each underlined noun with the correct direct object pronoun (*lo/la/los/las*).

1 ¿Compraste <u>el libro</u> ayer?

Sí, ... compré ayer.

2 ¿Siempre toma <u>la cena</u> a la hora exacta?

Sí, siempre .... toma a la hora exacta.

3 ¿Comiste <u>patatas fritas</u> calientes?

Sí, ... comí.

4 ¿Tu padrastro lavó <u>las verduras</u> esta mañana?

Sí, mi padrastro .... lavó esta mañana.

5 ¿Come <u>pasteles</u> a menudo?

No, no .... come a menudo.

6 ¿Tomas el <u>almuerzo</u> a mediodía?

No, ... tomo a las dos de la tarde.

G

Use a **direct object pronoun** to avoid repeating the noun. Remember that the direct object pronoun must agree with the noun it replaces, and it comes before the verb.

English	Spanish
me	me
you (singular)	te
him/her/it	lo/la
us	nos
you (plural)	os
them	los/las

3 Dani is taking about food and eating healthily. Rewrite each sentence, putting the words into the correct order.

1 la que comida Hay de región mi tomar

....

2 comer con calle puedes los en la La dedos

....

3 al Voy amigos semana con fines de restaurante mis los

....

4 bebida queremos café una tomamos en la un Si

....

5 porque es Generalmente no dientes malo para los como azúcar

....

6 sano Se en comer para necesita forma estar

....

4 Complete each sentence using a suitable infinitive from the box. There are more infinitives than gaps.

escribir jugar beber tener tomar comer estar hacer **H** evitar **H** sentir **H** probar **H** consistir

1 Hay que .... una dieta sana.

2 Se necesita .... mucha agua.

3 No hay que .... demasiadas patatas fritas.

4 Hay que .... ejercicio.

5 No se necesita .... la cena muy temprano.

6 Se necesita .... en forma.

H 7 Cuando vas a otro país, hace falta .... la comida en los puestos de la calle.

H 8 Si no te gusta la comida agria, pues ¡hay que ....la!

G

Impersonal verbs are followed by the infinitive.

hay que	you/one must
se necesita	you need / one needs
H ***hace falta***	you need to / one needs to

Hay que *comer bien.* ***Se necesita*** *practicar deporte.*

To make the impersonal verbs negative, add **no**.

no *hay que* ***no*** *se necesita* ***no*** *hace falta*

H 5 Complete this paragraph by translating the English words into Spanish.

Creo que tengo una dieta .... (*fairly healthy*). No como .... (*meat or fish*) porque soy vegetariano. Me gustan las cosas dulces, pero .... (*I only eat them*) a veces. Además, ... (*it is not necessary*) tomar bebidas con mucho azúcar. En mi opinión, hay que saber .... (*to eat well*) y esto también .... (*it helps you to have*) un cabello sano. Me gusta ir a restaurantes con amigos, pero .... (*we never go*) a lugares donde hay mucho humo.

Para mi amiga Leya, lo malo es que .... (*she cannot eat*) pan ni pasteles porque es alérgica. Leya no toma siempre el desayuno. Yo pienso que eso es malo porque lo tomo cada día y .... (*it gives me energy*) para el día en el colegio.

F 6 Translate these sentences into English.

1 Me gusta tomar la cena en casa. ....

2 Mi madre la suele preparar cada día. ....

3 Pero algunos días la hace mi padre. ....

4 Creo que se necesita tener una dieta sana y hacer ejercicio.

....

H 7 Translate this paragraph into Spanish.

There are many diverse dishes in Spanish-speaking countries. In Mexican towns it is normal to buy food in the street. I want to go there soon to try different types of Mexican food. Last year, I went to Spain and I ate a lot of fish. You need to avoid food full of sugar and have a healthy diet.

....

....

....

....

3 ¡Los tiempos cambian!

Using the imperfect tense • H Using *ya no* + verb

1 Circle the correct form of the imperfect tense to complete each sentence.

1 Cuando yo **era** / **eras** niño, **lloraba** / **llorabas** mucho.

2 En el pasado, tú **tenía** / **tenías** una vida bastante activa.

3 Tú **jugaba** / **jugabas** con tu hermano en el jardín.

4 Yo **ibas** / **iba** con mi madre al parque todos los días.

5 Yo solo **bebías** / **bebía** agua o leche.

6 Tú no **veías** / **veía** mucho la televisión.

G

Use the **imperfect tense** for saying what you used to do. The endings for **-er** and **-ir** verbs are the same.

	bailar	**comer**	**salir**
(yo)	bail**aba**	com**ía**	sal**ía**
(tú)	bail**abas**	com**ías**	sal**ías**
(él/ella/usted)	bail**aba**	com**ía**	sal**ía**
(nosotros/as)	bail**ábamos**	com**íamos**	sal**íamos**
(vosotros/as)	bail**abais**	com**íais**	sal**íais**
(ellos/ellas/ustedes)	bail**aban**	com**ían**	sal**ían**

These verbs are irregular in the imperfect:

ser (to be) → ***era, eras, era***
ir (to go) → ***iba, ibas, iba***
ver (to see/watch) → ***veía, veías, veía***
Remember the time phrases: ***antes, en el pasado*** + imperfect tense ***ahora*** + present tense

2 Which sentences are talking about the present and which about the past? Write 'present' or 'past' next to each sentence.

1 Oye música en la calle. ....

2 Comía muchos pasteles. ....

3 No jugaba al fútbol. ....

4 Corro en el parque. ....

5 Tomaba bebidas con azúcar. ....

6 No estaba en forma. ....

7 Tomo un buen desayuno. ....

8 Tengo mucha energía. ....

3 Find the mistakes in the verb tenses and write the correct forms.

1 Cuando era niña, paso mucho tiempo en mi cuarto. ....

2 Ahora yo hacía mucho deporte los fines de semana. ....

3 Ahora yo llevas una vida sana, digo yo. ....

4 Antes no duerme bien porque no hacía ejercicio físico. ....

5 En el pasado, no soy una persona muy activa y tengo una dieta malsana. ....

6 Ahora todos los días montaba en bicicleta con mis amigos. ....

H 7 Hace unos años, no me siento sana. ....

H 8 Hoy ibas mucho al gimnasio y estás en buena forma física. ....

4 Complete the sentences with the correct form of the imperfect tense using the verb in brackets.

1 En el pasado, ... (*ir*) al colegio en coche con mi padre.

2 Yo nunca .... (*hacer*) ejercicio.

3 Mi hermano .... (*ser*) más activo que yo.

4 Él .... (*jugar*) al fútbol en el parque.

5 Y tú, ¿.................... (*llevar*) una vida sana antes?

6 ¿Qué te .... (*gustar*) comer y beber?

H 7 Cuando yo era más joven, siempre estaba cansado. .... (*acostarse*) bastante temprano salvo durante las vacaciones.

H 8 Mi dieta .... (*consistir*) en muchas hamburguesas: no era sana.

H **5 Complete Andrea's blog with the correct form of the verb. Use the imperfect tense in the first paragraph and the present tense in the second. Think about the tense and the subject.**

1 Antes mi hermana y yo no .... una vida sana. .... comida dulce como pasteles y no .... deporte. Nos .... tarde, pero siempre .... cansadas. Mi hermano .... más energía que nosotras. Él .... al gimnasio con sus amigos tres veces a la semana.

2 Ahora mi hermana y yo ya no tomamos comida malsana. .... una dieta más equilibrada. Además, caminamos al colegio todos los días. Nuestro hermano .... todavía en forma y está orgulloso de nosotras. .... de nuestra salud: del cuerpo y de la mente.

F **6 Translate these sentences into Spanish.**

1 I like fresh food. ....

2 I have breakfast every day. ....

3 Before, I used to eat too many chips. ....

4 My father does a lot of exercise at weekends. ....

....

5 Now I have a healthy diet and I am more active. ....

....

H **7 Translate this paragraph into English.**

Cuando era más pequeño, tenía una dieta equilibrada. Ahora prefiero la comida malsana y no tomo suficiente agua. Sé que debo hacer más ejercicio y mejorar mi estilo de vida. Sin embargo, nadie me escucha cuando pido ayuda para dejar de fumar. Creo que hace falta cambiar el presente para tener un futuro mejor.

....

....

....

....

4 ¡Qué mal estoy!

- Using reflexive verbs in the preterite tense
- Giving advice using *debes, tienes que* and H *necesitas* + infinitive

1 Rewrite each sentence, putting the words into the correct order.

1 duelen oídos Me los mucho ....

2 ¿cabeza Te la duele? ....

3 un accidente ahora espalda la Tuve y duele me ....

4 nariz duelen boca la Le la y ....

G

Doler (to hurt) is a stem-changing verb. It works like **gustar** and **encantar**.

***Me** duel**e** el brazo.*	***Me** duel**en** los ojos.*
***Te** duel**e** la pierna.*	***Te** duel**en** los pies.*
*A mi madre **le** duel**e** la cabeza.*	*A mi madre **le** duel**en** los oídos.*

2 Complete these sentences with the correct form of *doler*.

1 Me .... la mano.

2 A mi padre le .... los dientes.

3 Me .... mucho la rodilla.

4 ¿Qué te pasa? ¿Te .... los dedos?

5 Mi mamá no está bien hoy. Le .... el estómago.

6 Te .... la garganta y no estás en forma.

G

Use the **preterite** tense to say what happened to you or what you did. Remember the accents – they are important in this tense!

	comprar	**comer**	**salir**
(yo)	compr**é**	com**í**	sal**í**
(tú)	compr**aste**	com**iste**	sal**iste**
(él/ella/usted)	compr**ó**	com**ió**	sal**ió**

For reflexive verbs like ***cortarse*** (to cut) and ***romperse*** (to break), use the correct reflexive pronoun before the verb and the definite article for the part of the body. In English we say 'my arm', but Spanish uses 'the arm'.

***Me** rompí el brazo.*	I broke my arm.
***Te** rompiste la pierna.*	You broke your leg.
*Alba **se** rompió el dedo.*	Alba broke her finger.

3 Complete these sentences with the correct form of the verb in brackets, using the correct pronoun if the verb is reflexive. Then translate the sentences into English.

1 Tú .... (*cortarse*) el dedo en la cocina.

....

2 Yo .... (*tener*) un accidente y ahora me duele la cabeza.

....

3 Antonio .... (*romperse*) el brazo la semana pasada.

....

4 ¿Tú .... (*romperse*) el pie?

....

H 5 Mi hermana .... (*caerse*) de la bicicleta en el jardín ayer.

....

H 6 Yo .... (*caerse*) en el parque.

....

4 Draw lines to match up the problems with the suitable advice.

1 Me duele la cabeza.
2 No me encuentro bien. Estoy muy cansado.
3 Me rompí el brazo.
4 Tengo un virus desde hace una semana.

a Tienes que ir al hospital.
b Debes pedir una cita con el doctor.
c Tienes que comprar medicina en la farmacia.
d Debes dormir un poco.

H Choose the most appropriate advice for each problem. There are more suggestions than you will need.

H 5 Tengo dolor de espalda desde hace tres días. ☐
H 6 Me quemé la piel de las piernas y me duele mucho. ☐

e Necesitas contestar el móvil. ¿No lo oyes? Está sonando.
f Tienes que descansar. Debes tener la piel suave.
g Necesitas evitar el sol e ir a la farmacia. No debes continuar así.
h Creo que debes ir a ver al médico.

G

To give someone advice, use ***debes*** or ***tienes que*** with an infinitive.

Debes *descansar en casa.* ***Tienes que*** *ir al doctor.*

H 5 Read this story about a recent accident. Complete each sentence with the appropriate verb(s).

El hijo de mis vecinos .... un accidente la semana pasada. Se .... de la bicicleta delante de un coche en la calle. Se .... el hombro y se .... al hospital.

Ahora se .... recuperando en casa. Todavía le .... mucho el hombro y no puede usar bien el brazo. Su madre le está cuidando la herida. El chico .... que relajarse y ya se .... un poco mejor.

F 6 Translate these sentences into English.

1 Hoy no me encuentro bien. ....

2 Me duele la cabeza y estoy cansado. ....

3 Mi padre necesita comprar medicinas en la farmacia.

....

4 La semana pasada me corté la mano en la cocina.

....

5 Cuando estoy enfermo, me quedo en la cama y duermo.

....

H 7 Translate this paragraph into Spanish on a separate sheet.

It is important to do exercise in order to be fit. Sometimes my legs hurt after running. Last month, I fell over and had to go straight to the hospital. If I have a temperature, I take medicine, stay at home and relax. You need to take care of your body and heart to live well.

5 Mi salud, de la cabeza a los pies

Using the simple future tense • Using 'if' clauses

1 Complete the sentences using the words in the box. There are more words than gaps.

llevaré	mejoraré	
haré	iré	lavaré
levantaré	pondré	
seré	tendré	

1 Hoy me levanto a las seis. Mañana me .... a las siete.

2 Normalmente hago los deberes en casa. Mañana los .... en la biblioteca.

3 Hoy tengo que estudiar. Mañana .... que hacer ejercicio.

4 Ahora como mucha comida malsana. En el futuro .... una vida más sana con una dieta más natural.

5 Normalmente voy a la cama a las nueve. El viernes .... a la cama a las diez.

G

Use the **simple future tense** to say what you will do. Add the endings to the infinitive of the verb.

mejorar (*to improve*)			
(*yo*)	mejorar**é**	(*nosotros/as*)	mejorar**emos**
(*tú*)	mejorar**ás**	(*vosotros/as*)	mejorar**éis**
(*él/ella/usted*)	mejorar**á**	(*ellos/as/ustedes*)	mejorar**án**

Some verbs have an irregular stem in the future tense.

decir → *diré* *poner* → *pondré* *salir* → *saldré*
hacer → *haré* *querer* → *querré* *tener* → *tendré*
poder → *podré* *saber* → *sabré* *venir* → *vendré*

Also remember ***habrá*** (there will be).

Use the correct reflexive pronoun with reflexive verbs: ***me*** *levantaré*, ***te*** *levantarás*, ***se*** *levantará*

2 Circle the correct verb form to complete each sentence.

1 Mi amiga **iré** / **irá** a España la semana próxima.

2 ¿Qué **hará** / **harás** tú el domingo próximo?

3 En abril yo **tendré** / **tendrás** que ir a casa de mis abuelos.

4 ¿A qué hora **comenzarás** / **comenzará** la fiesta el sábado?

5 En el futuro **cambiaré** / **cambiará** mi dieta para estar más sano.

6 Tú **practicará** / **practicarás** muchos deportes en el futuro.

G

Use the simple future tense in ***Si* clauses** to say what will happen if something else happens.

Si **+ present tense, future tense**
Si dejo *de fumar,* ***tendré*** *una vida más sana.*
If I stop smoking, I **will have** a healthier life.

3 Draw lines to match up the situation with how the person plans to make changes. Then translate the sentences into English on a separate sheet.

1 Si juego más al fútbol,
2 Si uso menos el móvil antes de ir a la cama,
3 Si comparto mi dinero con otra gente,
4 Si pido atención médica,
5 Si decido descansar más a menudo,

a mi salud mental mejorará.
b me llevarán al hospital.
c dormiré mejor.
d podré ser miembro del equipo del colegio.
e estaré muy feliz.

4 Read Manuel's blog. Fill in the gaps with the verbs in brackets. Decide whether you need to use the preterite, the imperfect or the future tense.

Cuando yo .... (*tener*) once años, no .... (*comer*) bien. .... (*haber*) siempre una gran cantidad de helados y pasteles en casa. Un día .... (*decidir*) cambiar mi vida: .... (*dejar*) de comer comida malsana y .... (*comenzar*) a hacer deporte cada día. Ahora soy una persona activa y sana, digo yo. Quiero mejorar mi salud mental en el futuro. Para eso, ... (*pasar*) menos tiempo en las redes sociales e .... (*ir*) temprano a la cama. Si la necesito .... (*pedir*) ayuda a mis padres o a mis profesores.

H Después de cambiar mis costumbres diarias, ... (*empezar*) a sentirme mejor poco a poco. También .... (*aumentar*) la cantidad de ejercicio que hacía. Después de unas semanas, ... (*sentirse*) mucho más en forma y .... (*estar*) más feliz. Gracias a los cambios que .... (*hacer*), creo que .... (*tener*) una vida mejor en el futuro.

H 5 Read what Alejandro says about his lifestyle. Fill in the gaps with a suitable verb. Think about the tense and the subject.

En mi opinión, ... que mejorar mi estilo de vida. El año pasado .... un montón de comida malsana y no .... ni un minuto haciendo ejercicio. .... imposible para mí sobrevivir sin café por la mañana. Cuando era pequeño, mi madre no me daba opciones en lo que .... comer. También .... más deporte porque jugaba al fútbol con mis amigos los domingos. Quiero tener más energía y, por supuesto, vivir muchos años. En mi opinión, si no .... demasiado café y no .... muchos dulces, te .... mejor. Por eso, en el futuro .... más ejercicio, ... ocho horas por la noche, ... la comida malsana y .... mucha agua.

Read the whole paragraph before you start. This will help you be sure who the subject is.

F 6 Translate these sentences into Spanish.

1 I do not feel well today. ....

2 I need to change my diet if I want to be fit. ....

3 My friend never eats unhealthy food. ....

4 To improve my health, I must do more sport. ....

5 Last week, I went swimming three times in the local pool.

....

H 7 Translate this paragraph into English.

Mi problema es que tengo malas costumbres. Cuando era joven, salía mucho con mis compañeros de clase. Ahora las horas que paso en las redes sociales están aumentando cada día. Si hago deporte con más frecuencia, esto me ayudará a cuidar mi salud mental. Hay muchos beneficios al cambiar de comportamiento y pasar tiempo al aire libre.

....

....

....

....

Glossary

bold = this word will appear in Higher exams only

aburrido	*bored, boring*
accidente (m)	*accident*
acostarse	*(to) go to bed*
activo	*active*
además	*also, besides, as well*
agrio	*sour*
agua (f)	*water*
alérgico	*allergic*
alguno	*a/an, any (m)*
alguno	*one, some (of them) (for plural noun)*
almuerzo (m)	*lunch*
arroz (m)	*rice*
así	*like this, like that*
atención	*attention*
aumentar	*(to) increase*
azúcar (m)	*sugar*
bebida (f)	*drink, beverage*
beneficio (m)	*benefit, profit*
boca (f)	*mouth*
brazo (m)	*arm*
cabello (m)	*hair*
cabeza (f)	*head*
cada	*each, every*
caer(se)	*(to) fall*
café (m)	*coffee, café*
caliente	*hot*
cambiar; cambiarse	*(to) change, exchange; (to) get changed*
caminar	*(to) walk*
camino (m)	*path, way, route*
cansado	*tired, tiring*
cantidad (f)	*quantity, amount*
carne (f)	*meat*
cayó	*(she, he, it, you (sing formal)) fell*

cena (f)	*dinner*
chileno	*Chilean*
chocolate (m)	*chocolate*
churros (mpl)	*churros*
cita (f)	*appointment, date*
cocina (f)	*kitchen, cuisine, cooking*
comenzar	*(to) start, begin*
comer	*(to) eat | eating*
comida (f)	*food, meal*
compartir	*(to) share*
consistir (en)	*(to) consist (of)*
corazón (m)	*heart*
correr	*(to) run | running*
cortar(se)	*(to) cut (oneself)*
cuarto (m)	*room, bedroom, quarter*
cubano	*Cuban*
cuchara (f)	*spoon*
cuchillo (m)	*knife*
cuerpo (m)	*body*
cuidado (m)	*care, carefulness*
decidir	*(to) decide*
dedo (m)	*finger*
dejar; dejar de + inf.	*(to) leave, allow; (to) stop + verb (-ing)*
demasiado	*too much, too many*
desde	*from, since*
despertar(se)	*(to) wake up*
después; **después de (+infinitive)**	*after, afterwards;* ***after (+ -ing)***
diario	*daily*
diente (m)	*tooth*
dieta (f)	*diet*
digo	*(I) say, tell | am saying, telling*

diré	*(I) will say, tell / am going to say, tell*
directamente	*directly, straight away*
diría	*(I) would say, tell*
diverso	*diverse*
doler	*(to) hurt*
dolor (m)	*pain, ache*
dulce	*sweet*
ejercicio (m)	*exercise*
energía (f)	*energy*
enfermo	*ill, sick*
entrante (m)	*starter*
entre	*between, among*
equilibrado	*balanced*
era	*(I, she, he, it, one) was / used to be / (you (sing formal)) were / used to be*
eras	*(you (sing informal)) were / used to be*
espalda (f)	*back (body part)*
especialmente	*mainly, especially*
estaba	*(I, she, he, it, one) was / used to be / (you (sing formal)) were / used to be*
estás	*(you (sing informal)) are / are being*
estómago (m)	*stomach*
evitar	*(to) avoid*
exactamente	*exactly*
exacto	*exact*
farmacia (f)	*pharmacy, chemist's*
fiebre (f)	*fever*
físico	*physical*
fresco	*fresh, cool, chilly*
fruta (f)	*fruit*
fumar	*(to) smoke*
garganta (f)	*throat*
generalmente	*generally*
gimnasio (m)	*gym*
gracias	*thank you, thanks*
hace falta (+ infinitive)	*it's necessary (to)*
hace; hace (dos años)	*it is (+ weather noun or adjective); (two years) ago*
hambre (f)	*hunger, famine*
hamburguesa (f)	*burger, hamburger*
haré	*(I) will do, make / am going to do, make*
helado (m)	*ice cream*
herida (f)	*injury, wound*
hispanohablante	*Spanish-speaking*
hoja (f)	*sheet, leaf*
hombro (m)	*shoulder*
hospital (m)	*hospital*
hoy	*today*
huevo (m)	*egg*
humo (m)	*smoke*
iba; **me iba (de), se iba (de)**	*(I, she, he, it, one) used to go / was going / you (sing formal)) used to go / were going;* ***used to leave / was leaving / used to leave / were leaving***
ibas; **te ibas (de)**	*(you (sing informal)) used to go / were going;* ***used to leave / were leaving***
idea (f)	*idea*
inglés	*English*
joven (mf)	*young person*
lavar; lavarse	*(to) wash; (to) wash (oneself), have a wash*

leche (f)	*milk*			
levantarse	*(to) get up*			
ligero	*light*			
lleno	*full, filled*			
llorar	*(to) cry*			
lo que	*what, that which (subj)*			
malsano	*unhealthy*			
mano (f)	*hand*			
me	*me (obj) | (to) me (indirect obj) | myself (reflex)*			
medicina (f)	*medicine, medication*			
médico (m)	*doctor*			
medio	*half*			
mediodía (m)	*noon, midday*			
mejorar	*(to) improve*			
mental	*mental*			
mente (f)	*mind*			
merienda (f)	*afternoon snack*			
mexicano, mejicano	*Mexican*			
minuto (m)	*minute*			
montón (m)	*a lot, pile*			
mover(se)	*(to) move*			
natural	*natural*			
niño (m)	*child, (young) boy*			
no	*no, not*			
normal	*normal, usual, regular*			
nos	*us (obj) | (to) us (indirect obj) | (to) ourselves (reflex) | (to) each other (recip)*			
oído (m)	*ear, hearing*			
oigo	*(I) hear | am hearing*			
oír	*(to) hear*			
olor (m)	*smell*			
opción (f)	*option, choice*			
orgulloso	*proud*			
os	*you (pl informal) (obj) | (to) you (indirect obj) | (to) yourselves (reflex) | (to) each other (recip)*			
oye	*(she, he, it, one) hears | (you (sing formal)) hear | is hearing are hearing*			
oyes	*(you (sing informal)) hear | are hearing*			
pan (m)	*bread*			
parecer; parecerse a	*(to) seem; (to) look like*			
pasado (m)	*past*			
pasta (f)	*pasta*			
pastel (m)	*cake*			
patatas fritas (fpl)	*chips*			
peruano	*Peruvian*			
pescado (m)	*fish*			
pie (m); a pie	*foot; on foot, walking*			
piel (f)	*skin, fur, leather*			
pierna (f)	*leg*			
(un) poco	*not much / little*			
podré	*(I) will be able to | am going to be able to*			
pondré; me pondré	*(I) will put | am going (to) put; will put (on), get, become | am going to put (on), get, become*			
por	*by, for, through,* ***around, because of****, in, at, per*			
postre (m)	*dessert*			
práctica (f)	*practice*			
practicar	*(to) practise*			
presente (m)	*present*			

probar	*(to) try, taste, try on*			
pronto	*soon, early*			
puesto (m)	*position, stall, stand, place*			
¿Qué te pasa?	*What's wrong?*			
querré	*(I) will want, love*			
queso (m)	*cheese*			
recuperar; recuperarse	*(to) get (something) back; (to) recover, get better*			
rodilla (f)	*knee*			
romper(se)	*(to) break*			
saber	*(to) know (how to)*			
sabré	*(I) will know (how to)*			
saldré	*(I) will go out, leave*			
salud (f)	*health*			
salvo	*except for, but*			
sano	*healthy, wholesome*			
se	*himself, herself, itself, oneself, yourself (formal) (reflex)* ***| themselves (reflex) | yourselves (formal) (reflex) | (to) each other (recip)***			
se necesita	*you need (to) (general), one needs (to)*			
sed (f)	*thirst*			
sentir; sentirse	*(to) regret, sense; (to) feel*			
siesta (f)	*afternoon nap*			
simple	*straightforward*			
sobrevivir	*(to) survive*			
sonar	*(to) sound, ring*			
suave	*soft, gentle, mild*			
suficiente	*enough*			
te	*you (sing informal) (obj) | (to) you (indirect obj) | yourself (reflex)*			
té (m)	*tea*			
temprano	*early*			
tendré; tendré que	*(I) will have | am going to have; will have to | am going to have to*			
tenedor (m)	*fork*			
tener ... años	*to be ... years old*			
tenías; tenías que	*(you (sing informal)) had | used to have | were having; had to | used to have to | were having to*			
variedad (f)	*variety*			
vegano	*vegan*			
vegetariano	*vegetarian*			
veía	*(I, she, he, it, one) used to see, watch | was seeing, watching | (you) used to see, watch | were seeing, watching*			
veías	*(you (sing informal)) used to see, watch | were seeing, watching*			
vendré	*(I) will come*			
verano (m)	*summer*			
verdura (f)	*vegetable*			
vestir; vestirse	*(to) wear, dress; (to) get dressed*			
viejo	*old, aged*			
virus (m)	*virus*			
y media (f)	*half-past*			
y, e	*and, past (time)*			
ya no	*no longer, no more*			

Zona de cultura La vida escolar en España

Using absolute superlatives

1 Circle the correct adjective to complete each sentence.

1 Para ir al colegio llevo una camisa **blanco / blanca**, un pantalón **azul / azules** y unos zapatos **negros / negras**.

2 En algunos institutos privados los alumnos tienen que llevar una corbata **verde / verdes** o **rojo / roja**.

3 En la escuela de mi hermana los chicos llevan una camiseta **gris / grises** con un pantalón y las chicas llevan una falda **azul / azula** con un jersey.

4 Me encantaría llevar unas zapatillas de deporte **blancas / blanco** para ir al colegio, pero tengo que llevar unos zapatos **aburridos / aburrido**.

H 5 No tenemos uniforme y por eso suelo llevar un vestido **negro / negros** con una chaqueta **cómodas / cómoda**.

2 Complete the questions using words from the box and write the correct letter to match up the questions with the answers.

edificio año termina ropa comida

1 ¿Qué .... llevas en el instituto? ☐

2 ¿Cuándo comienza el .... escolar? ☐

3 ¿Cuándo ....? ☐

4 ¿Te gusta la ....? ☐

5 ¿Cómo es el ....? ☐

a Tenemos una biblioteca moderna, pero el patio es pequeño.

b Siempre termina la tercera semana de junio.

c Normalmente llevo un pantalón o una falda.

d Sí, está rica. El precio de los bocadillos es barato también.

e Siempre comienza la segunda semana de septiembre.

3 Complete the missing words in the parallel translations.

1	En mi .... hay más de ciento cincuenta	On my course there are more than .... pupils.
2	El comienzo del .... escolar es divertido en muchos colegios.	The .... of the school year is fun in .... schools.
3	En el pasado, el uniforme .... era común, pero ahora .... estudiantes pueden decidir qué llevar.	In the past, school .... was common, but now many students can .... what to wear.
4	En .... colegios hay por lo menos .... clases al	In some schools .... at least six .... a day.

G

When using 'really' or 'extremely' before an adjective in Spanish, use the **absolute superlative**.

Add ***-ísimo/a(s)*** at the end of the adjective. Remove the final vowel from the adjective if it has one.

bueno/a(s) → *buen**ísimo**, buen**ísima**, buen**ísimos**, buen**ísimas***

difícil(es) → *dificil**ísimo**, dificil**ísima**, dificil**ísimos**, dificil**ísimas***

The adjective should agree with the noun it is describing.

*El director es estrict**ísimo**.*	The headteacher is **extremely/really strict**.
*Las profesoras son divertid**ísimas**.*	The (female) teachers are **extremely/really fun**.

4 Rewrite each sentence using the correct absolute superlative form of the adjective in brackets.

1 Las clases son .... (*aburrido*).
2 El patio es .... (*grande*).
3 Mi curso de español es .... (*importante*).
H 4 La formación profesional es .... (*popular*).
H 5 Las instalaciones son .... (*bueno*).
H 6 Incluso los profesores son .... (*alegre*).

F 5 Translate these sentences into Spanish.

1 I think that my school is modern. ....

Think about the word order.

2 We wear black trousers and white shirts. ....
3 The school year always starts in September. ....
4 In my opinion, the food in my school is extremely bad. ....

....

5 In some schools the pupils do not wear ties or jackets. ....

....

H 6 Translate this paragraph into English.

Asisto a un instituto público en una ciudad grandísima. En mi opinión, las instalaciones son decepcionantes, pero la directora es buenísima. Mientras que la mayoría de los colegios en mi zona tienen uniforme, yo puedo llevar mi propia ropa. Me gusta la ropa deportiva porque es cómoda, aunque la semana pasada llevé un vestido azul oscuro.

....

....

....

....

1 Un día en el insti

F Forming questions

1 Fill in the missing letters to complete the days of the week and subjects in Karima's diary.

1 Los l_ _ _ _ estudio ciencias e hi_ _ _ _ _ _.
2 Los m_ _ _ _ _, si no tengo deberes, voy al club de te_ _ _ _.
3 Los mi_ _ _ _ _ _ _ tengo clase de tec_ _ _ _ _ _ _.
4 Los j_ _ _ _ _ a las diez y cuarto tengo di_ _ _ _.

G

Question words are important in Spanish. The verb often follows the question word. Remember: all question words have an accent.

¿**Qué**?	What?
¿**Cuál**?	Which?
¿**Cuándo**?	When?
¿**Cuánto/a(s)**?	How many?
¿**Cómo**?	How?
¿**Dónde**?	Where?
¿**Quién**?	Who?

When followed by a noun, ¿**Qué**? means 'Which?'
¿***Qué*** *actividad haces los martes?*
Which activity do you do on Tuesdays?
Remember that ¿***Cuánto/a(s)***? agrees with the noun.
¿***Cuántos*** *descansos tienes?*
How many breaks do you have?

2 Complete the questions with the correct question word.

1 ¿.............. es la exposición de arte? El jueves.
2 ¿.............. asignatura prefieres? Prefiero la música porque toco un instrumento y canto.
3 ¿.............. vas al instituto? Normalmente voy a pie, si hace buen tiempo.
4 ¿.............. vas al club de baloncesto? A las tres y cuarto cada martes.
5 ¿.............. es tu profesor favorito? Me gusta mucho el profesor de español.
6 ¿.............. haces en el patio? Siempre juego al fútbol o hablo con mis amigos.

3 Read the blog and translate the underlined phrases.

Me encanta mi colegio en Barcelona porque **1** no tenemos deberes y la mayoría de los alumnos son simpáticos. **2** Cada día voy al colegio en autobús con mi amigo español, que se llama Iván. Mis clases comienzan a las ocho y **3** terminan a las dos y media. Siempre voy a la biblioteca **4** durante la hora de comer, pero en este momento está cerrada y **5** salimos al patio durante el descanso. **6** Las asignaturas que más me gustan son la religión y las matemáticas.

1 ....
2 ....
3 ....
4 ....
5 ....
6 ....

4 Translate these sentences into English on a separate sheet.

1 Las clases de natación duran cuarenta minutos.
2 A veces trabajo en la radio escolar.
3 Vimos varios vídeos en historia, pero ninguno fue interesante.
4 Fue un momento especial cuando bailamos en una competición nacional.
5 Solamente vamos a la biblioteca si las clases terminan temprano.

1 Un día en el insti

H Using the relative pronouns *que, donde, cuando*

H 1 Write the correct letter in the box to match up the sentence halves. Then translate each sentence into English.

1 Cuando llueve, siempre voy ☐
2 Llevo un año jugando ☐
3 Solo llevamos tres meses ☐
4 Creo que ser miembro de un club ☐

a estudiando drama en el club de teatro.
b al colegio en coche.
c te anima a desarrollar tus ideas.
d al fútbol y soy capitán del equipo.

....

....

....

....

H 2 Circle the correct relative pronoun to complete each sentence.

1 Prefiero los miércoles **cuando** / **donde** tengo deporte porque soy la capitana.
2 Hice una entrevista con el director **cuando** / **que** organicé un espectáculo.
3 Hay una biblioteca maravillosa **que** / **donde** siempre hago mis deberes.
4 Acabo de empezar en el club de baile **donde** / **cuando** aprendí un baile urbano.
5 Estudio las asignaturas artísticas **donde** / **que** desarrollan tu confianza.

G

H Use the **relative pronouns *que*** (that/which/who), ***donde*** (where) or ***cuando*** (when) to give more information about the noun you are talking about.

*Voy a estudiar matemáticas, **que** es mi asignatura preferida.*
I am going to study maths, **which** is my favourite subject.

*Prefiero las clases de inglés **cuando** no tengo que escribir mucho.*
I prefer English lessons **when** I don't have to write much.

*Hay unas instalaciones maravillosas **donde** podemos practicar deportes.*
There are some wonderful facilities **where** we can do sport.

H 3 Complete each sentence with the correct relative pronoun (*cuando*, *donde* or *que*).

1 Voy a la escuela en tren .... no tengo tiempo para andar.
2 Tengo que llevar una falda azul claro, ... no es muy cómoda.
3 Mi mejor amigo siempre va a la biblioteca, ... lee muchas novelas.
4 Hay mucho ruido en el patio .... todos los estudiantes están allí.

H 4 Translate this paragraph into Spanish on a separate sheet.

I only walk to school when it is good weather. However, sometimes it is too hot, with temperatures above 30 degrees. The facilities where we study are excellent because they have just built a new building. I like to play in the school orchestra where I can make friends.

2 ¿Qué tal tus estudios?

F Talking about the opinions of others

1 Circle the correct verb and adjective to complete the opinions. Then translate each sentence into English.

1 **No me gusta / No me gustan** la historia, ya que es **duro / dura / duros / duras**.

....

2 **Me gusta / Me gustan** las lenguas porque son **divertido / divertida / divertidos / divertidas**.

....

3 **Me encanta / Me encantan** la educación física porque es **fácil / fáciles**.

....

4 **No me gusta / Me gustan** nada el dibujo porque es **aburrido / aburrida / aburridos / aburridas**.

....

2 Underline the English words in this tangled translation and then write out the text in Spanish.

Mi asignatura favourite son science porque me interesa mucho nature. I hate las matemáticas because son imposibles y la profesora always nos da muchos homework. I have un examen de English pronto y it is hard recordar las words. Voy a learn de mis errores porque I want mejorar mi level.

....

....

....

....

....

....

G To talk about other people's opinions with verbs like *gustar*, *encantar* and *interesar*, change the **pronoun**.

me *gusta(n)*	**I** like	**le** *gusta(n)*	**he/she** likes
te *gusta(n)*	**you** like	**les** *gusta(n)*	**they** like

Use the word ***a*** when mentioning a person.
***A** mi hermana <u>le</u> interesa la música.*

3 Complete the sentences with the correct pronoun and form of the verb in brackets.

1 A Emilio .... (*like*) la tecnología porque es fácil.

2 A mis amigos .... (*love*) los deportes como el baloncesto.

3 ¿A ti .... (*like*) los ordenadores?

4 A mi novia .... (*like*) religión porque es interesante.

5 A mi profesor de español .... (*be interested in*) la historia de España.

Remember that when giving an opinion with a noun, you need the **definite article** (*el, la, los, las*): *Me encantan* ***las*** *matemáticas.*

4 Translate these sentences into Spanish on a separate sheet.

1 I am interested in PE.

2 My sister likes art a lot.

3 She is going to pass the languages exam.

4 I am going to read the text and questions in silence.

5 I listened to the history teacher and I wrote the dates.

2 ¿Qué tal tus estudios?

H Using *lo que*

H 1 Complete the sentences with a word from the box and translate each sentence into English.

pesada
miedo
estudios
prácticos
da

1 Prefiero estudiar los idiomas porque son .... y fáciles.

....

2 Odio el teatro porque tengo .... de actuar en el escenario.

....

3 Lo que más me gusta es la música clásica porque nunca es ....

....

4 Se me .... bien el inglés porque tengo un gran profesor.

....

5 Mis .... son importantes, pero a veces saco malas notas en historia porque no recuerdo todas las fechas.

....

G

H Use ***lo que*** to mean 'what' when you are <u>not</u> asking a question.

Lo que *menos me gusta es el inglés porque se me da mal.*
What I like least is English because I am bad at it.

No saben ***lo que*** *van a servir para comer esta tarde.*
They don't know what they are going to eat this afternoon.

H 2 Write the correct letter to match up the sentence halves and translate each sentence into English on a separate sheet.

1 Lo que más me ☐
2 No sabemos lo que ☐
3 Lo que más me interesa ☐
4 A veces no me interesa ☐
5 Creo que lo que menos ☐

a es la biblioteca nueva que van a construir.
b me gusta es que nos ponen muchas pruebas.
c gusta es entregar mis tareas a tiempo.
d lo que dice mi profesora sobre las obras de teatro.
e vamos a hacer después del instituto.

H 3 Finish these phrases by using a future tense verb from the box to create sentences about intentions.

aprenderé	haré	preguntaré	estudiaré	participaré	asistiré

1 Para aprobar mis exámenes, *preguntaré al profesor si no entiendo.* ....
2 Para resolver los problemas complejos, ...
3 Para poder contestar más preguntas en clase, ...
4 Para tener éxito, ...

H 4 Translate this paragraph into English on a separate sheet.

No me gusta el instituto. Ayer hablé con mi profesor y resolví unos problemas serios. Muchas asignaturas son complejas y lo que menos me gusta son las ciencias porque son muy difíciles. A mi amigo Mario le gustan los números. Para mejorar, escucharé más en clase y conservaré mis libros para estudiar antes de los exámenes.

3 ¿Cómo cambiarías tu instituto?

Using the conditional tense

1 Write the correct letter to create a list of school rules.

Las reglas de nuestro instituto

IES López Blanco

1 Se puede beber ☐
2 Está prohibido usar ☐
3 Se debe quedar ☐
4 Debemos respetar ☐
5 Se debe trabajar ☐
6 Hay que ☐

a a los alumnos y a los profesores.
b agua en clase.
c aceptar las diferencias.
d tu teléfono móvil en el colegio.
e sentado en clase.
f bien en grupos.

2 Complete the sentences with an appropriate verb in the conditional tense from the box.

Bajaría	Mejoraría	Pondría	Reduciría
Habría	Cambiaría	Daría	

1 .... muchas normas en mi colegio porque no estoy de acuerdo con algunas.

2 .... el precio de las chaquetas porque son muy caras.

3 .... más descansos en el patio durante el día escolar.

4 .... ordenadores a los alumnos en cada clase.

H 5 .... la calidad de la comida porque mucha comida acaba en la basura.

H 6 .... más profesores en el patio porque algunos alumnos gritan demasiado y otros amenazan o sufren amenazas.

G

Use the **conditional tense** to say what you would do. To form the conditional tense, add the imperfect tense endings of **-er**/**-ir** verbs to the <u>infinitive</u>.

*acepta**ría*** I would accept
*ir**ías*** you would go
*come**ría*** he/she would eat

Some verbs have an irregular stem:

hacer → ***har**ía* (I would do)
poner → ***pondr**ía* (I would put)
tener → ***tendr**ía* (I would have)

The conditional of *hay* (there is/are) is ***habría*** (there would be).

3 Complete the sentences with the correct form of the conditional of the verb in brackets. Then translate each sentence into English on a separate sheet.

1 .... (*cambiar – I*) la actitud seria de algunos de los profesores.

2 No .... (*tener – I*) muchos deberes.

H 3 .... (*convencer – I*) a los profesores de mejorar el horario.

H 4 Además, los profesores .... (*ofrecer – they*) más actividades y menos tareas.

4 Complete the sentences with the conditional form of the verb given in English in brackets.

1 Para mejorar el instituto, ... (*I would paint*) el edificio.

2 .... (*I would open*) una sala de juegos para los estudiantes.

H 3 Para mejorar mi español, ... (*I would repeat*) las palabras para aprenderlas.

H 4 Siempre .... (*I would allow*) el uso de los móviles para conseguir información.

G

Here is the full conjugation of the **conditional** tense of ***ser*** (to be).

*ser**ía***	I would be	*ser**íamos***	we would be
*ser**ías***	you would be	*ser**íais***	you (plural) would be
*ser**ía***	he/she/it would be	*ser**ían***	they would be

Other **irregular stems**:

decir	→	***dir**ía*	*saber*	→	***sabr**ía*
poder	→	***podr**ía*	*salir*	→	***saldr**ía*
querer	→	***querr**ía*	*venir*	→	***vendr**ía*

H **5 For each opinion about school, write a suggestion for how to improve it. Use the verbs in the box.**

cambiar permitir reducir mejorar pintar mantener

Mantener is irregular like ***tener***.

1 No hay muchas actividades distintas.

Mejoraría la cantidad de actividades.

2 Estoy en contra de gastar mucho dinero en el uniforme.

....

3 El patio está en mal estado.

....

4 La biblioteca no está limpia.

....

F **6 Translate these sentences into English.**

1 Está prohibido llegar tarde a clase. ....

2 Mi amigo tiene miedo en el patio. ....

3 En mi instituto cambiaría la biblioteca porque es vieja.

....

4 En clase sólo se puede beber agua.

....

5 Siempre aprendemos la importancia del respeto.

....

F **7 Translate this paragraph into Spanish.**

I spend a lot of money on school food. The bad thing is that there are few options and the burgers are bad. To improve my school, I would reduce the cost of the sandwiches. Two days ago I attended a maths club, where we would learn more with our personal electronic devices.

....

....

....

....

4 La gente de mi insti

Using negatives

1 Read these sentences about study skills. Are these skills good or bad? Write the number for each sentence on the correct line.

☺ .... ☹ ....

1 Nunca olvido mi bolígrafo.
2 No hago nada.
3 Me encanta aprender.
4 Nunca leo libros.
5 Estudio mucho para los exámenes.
6 No soy muy organizada.
7 Siempre salgo de casa tarde.
8 Soy muy trabajador e independiente.
9 No escucho a nadie.
10 Siempre llevo mis cuadernos.

G

Many **negative expressions** form a 'sandwich' around the verb:

No *escribo* ***nada****.*	I **don't** write **anything**.
No *hablo con* ***nadie****.*	I **don't** talk to **anyone**.
No *voy a* ***ningún*** *club.*	I **don't** go to **any** clubs.
No *tengo* ***ninguna*** *clase divertida.*	I **don't** have **any** fun classes.

Nunca can also go before the verb.

Nunca *llego a tiempo. /* ***No*** *llego* ***nunca*** *a tiempo.* — I **never** arrive on time.

H ***Jamás*** works in the same way.

Jamás *falto a clase. /* ***No*** *falto* ***jamás*** *a clase.* — I **never** miss class.

2 Change each sentence into the opposite by using negative expressions.

1 Escucho a todos. *No escucho a nadie.*
2 Siempre escucho música. ....
3 Me gustan todas las actividades. ....
4 Hago mucho. ....
5 Llevo bolígrafos a clase. ....

3 Write the correct letter to match up the questions with the answers.

1 ¿Escuchas en clase? ☐
2 ¿Te llevas bien con tus profesores? ☐
3 ¿Cómo te preparas para los exámenes? ☐
H 4 ¿Dónde sueles ir después del colegio? ☐
H 5 ¿Qué haces si faltas a clase? ☐

a Leo mis libros y escribo en mi cuaderno.
b Cuando no estoy presente, pregunto a un compañero qué me perdí.
c Sí, porque la mayoría son agradables.
d Depende. Voy al parque o, si llueve, vuelvo a casa temprano.
e Siempre escucho porque quiero sacar buenas notas.

4 Tick the box to identify conditional statements that refer to an ideal teacher rather than an actual teacher. Then translate each sentence into English.

1 Me llevo bien con mi profesora porque es trabajadora. ☐

....

2 Pone muchos deberes y no me deja comer en clase. ☐

....

3 Sería simpático y me dejaría escuchar música. ☐

....

H 4 Siempre tiene un buen sentido del humor y nunca está enfadado. ☐

....

H 5 Jamás nos deja hablar mucho en clase o usar nuestros móviles. ☐

....

H 6 Tendría una sonrisa increíble y no gritaría nunca. ☐

....

To help recognise the conditional tense for regular verbs, remember that the endings are added to the infinitive of each verb: *hablar* → *hablar**ía***.

F **5 Translate these sentences into Spanish.**

1 I never arrive late. ....

2 She does not listen to anyone. ....

3 He does not let me eat or drink in class. ....

4 I don't do any activities after school. ....

5 A perfect student would listen and study a lot.

....

H **6 Translate this paragraph into English.**

No soy un buen alumno. Ayer no me callé en clase y no saqué buenas notas en la prueba. Normalmente tengo una actitud positiva hacia las tareas porque el profesor me ayuda a mejorar mi trabajo y no nos trata como niños pequeños. Siempre aprendemos mucho porque crea un ambiente agradable.

Translate this pronoun as 'us'.
Think carefully about the word order.

....

....

....

....

5 El viaje de fin de curso

Using adjectives and adverbs

1 Fill each gap with the correct adverb from the box.

simplemente
rápidamente
verdaderamente
perfectamente
recientemente
seguramente

1 .... (*recently*) mis amigos y yo hicimos un viaje a Madrid.

2 El primer día salimos del hotel .... (*quickly*) para ir al centro.

3 El hotel estaba .... (*perfectly*) limpio y tenía una piscina pequeña.

4 El centro de Madrid era .... (*simply*) increíble y tenía muchas tiendas buenas.

5 El viaje fue .... (*truly*) especial y .... (*certainly*) volvería a Madrid algún día.

2 Complete the missing verbs in the parallel translations.

1	Recientemente fuimos a un .... grande con mi clase.	.... we went to a .... museum with my class.
2	El segundo día .... muchos .... históricos.	On the second day we visited lots of .... monuments.
3	.... tercer día .... sol y vimos un .... maravilloso.	On the .... day it was .... and .... a wonderful lake.
4	...................., mi amiga Amira .... su ...., pero una señora lo encontró.	Unfortunately, my .... Amira lost her book, but a .... found it.
5	El .... fue completamente .... porque me divertí y .... mucho.	The trip was .... perfect because I .... myself and I learnt ....

G

Remember that **adjectives** usually go after the noun they describe: *un lago* ***pequeño***.

Some go before the noun (***mucho***, ***poco***, ***próximo***, ***último***): *había* ***pocas*** *actividades*.

Some are shortened before a masculine singular noun (***primer***, ***tercer***, ***buen***, ***mal***, ***algún***, ***ningún***): *el* ***tercer*** *día*.

Grande becomes ***gran*** before a singular noun and its meaning changes from 'big' to 'great': *un* ***gran*** viaje (a great trip).

Único means 'only' before the noun and 'unique' after the noun.

3 Rewrite each sentence using the English adjective in brackets, putting it in the right place in the sentence.

1 Aprendimos sobre la comida. (*traditional*)

....

2 Fuimos a una playa. (*big*)

....

3 Había gente en el parque. (*few*)

....

H 4 También visitamos unos lugares. (*typical*)

....

H 5 Pienso que fue un éxito. (*great*)

....

G

Adverbs are used to say when, where or how something is done. In English, many adverbs end in '-ly'.

Add ***-mente*** to the feminine form of the adjective to form the **adverb** in Spanish.

completo → completa → completamente
reciente → reciente → recientemente
real → realmente

4 Complete each sentence with the Spanish translation of the English word or words in brackets.

1 Compré una corbata .... (*absolutely unique*).

2 Fue un momento .... (*really bad*) cuando perdimos el autobús.

3 La cuarta noche comimos una paella que estuvo ....
(*simply wonderful*).

H 4 Disfrutamos del día entero hasta .... (*approximately*) las seis.

H **5 Read the text and underline the 6 mistakes. Then write out the text in Spanish, correcting the errors.**

El viaje escolar que hicimos reciente fue maravillosa. El primero día fuimos a un lago e hicimos actividades deportivas. El segunda día fue completa diferente porque visitamos un museo. En conclusión, fue una increíble experiencia y voy a guardar cada segundo en mi memoria para siempre.

F **6 Translate these sentences into English.**

1 Prefiero los viajes con mi clase. ....

2 Normalmente hacemos muchas actividades divertidas.

....

3 Recientemente fuimos a un bosque único. ....

4 Desafortunadamente, no hizo buen tiempo, pero aprendimos mucho.

....

5 Me gustaría volver al museo porque es realmente maravilloso.

....

F **7 Translate this paragraph into Spanish on a separate sheet.**

Translate this using the adjective *escolar*. What ending does it need?

School trips are exciting. The teachers are happy and we can visit different places. Recently we went on a cultural trip. I am not interested in history, but there was a truly enormous monument and I loved it. I would like to return there because the city has some wonderful shops.

Glossary

bold = this word will appear in Higher exams only

Spanish	English	😐	🙂	😎
abrir	*(to) open | opening*			
aceptar	*(to) accept | accepting*			
actitud (f)	*attitude*			
acuerdo (m), de acuerdo	*agreement, in agreement*			
alegre	*lively, cheerful, happy*			
alumno (m), alumna (f)	*pupil, student*			
amenaza (f)	*threat*			
amenazar	*(to) threaten | threatening*			
animar	*(to) encourage, cheer up | encouraging, cheering up*			
aprender	*(to) learn | learning*			
aprobar	*(to) pass | passing*			
arte (m)	*art*			
artístico	*artistic*			
asignatura (f)	*subject*			
asistir (a)	*(to) attend | attending*			
Barcelona (f)	*Barcelona*			
basura (f)	*rubbish, litter, junk*			
biblioteca (f)	*library*			
blanco	*white*			
bolígrafo (m)	*pen*			
callarse	*(to) be quiet, keep quiet | being quiet, keeping quiet*			
camisa (f)	*shirt*			
camiseta (f)	*T-shirt*			
cantar	*(to) sing | singing*			
capitán (m)	*captain*			
capitana (f)	*captain*			
chaqueta (f)	*jacket*			
ciencia (f), ciencias (fpl)	*science*			
claro	*clear, light (in colour)*			
clase (f)	*classroom, class, lesson*			
colegio (m)	*school, high school*			
comienzo (m)	*start, beginning*			
competición (f)	*competition, contest*			
complejo	*complex, complicated*			
completamente	*completely*			
completo	*complete, full*			
conclusión (f)	*conclusion*			
conseguir	*(to) acquire, obtain, get | acquiring, obtaining, getting*			
conservar	*(to) preserve, conserve | preserving, conserving*			
construir	*(to) build | building*			
contestar	*(to) answer | answering*			
(en) contra	*against*			
convencer	*(to) convince, persuade | convincing, persuading*			
corbata (f)	*tie*			
cuaderno (m)	*notebook, workbook*			
cuarto	*fourth*			
curso (m)	*school year, course*			
deberes (mpl)	*homework, duties*			
decepcionante	*disappointing*			
decir	*(to) say, tell | saying, telling*			
depender (de)	*(to) depend (on) | depending (on)*			
deportivo	*sports*			

desafortunadamente	*unfortunately*			
descanso (m)	*break, interval, rest*			
desarrollar	*(to) develop | developing*			
dibujo (m)	*drawing*			
diferencia (f)	*difference*			
distinto	*different*			
drama (m)	*drama*			
durar	*(to) last, take | lasting, taking*			
duro	*hard, harsh*			
edificio (m)	*building*			
empezar	*(to) begin, start | beginning, starting*			
en este momento	*at the moment*			
entero	*entire, whole, complete*			
entregar	*(to) deliver, submit | delivering, submitting*			
entrevista (f)	*interview*			
error (m)	*mistake, error*			
escenario (m)	*stage*			
escolar	*school*			
escribir	*(to) write | writing*			
escuela (f)	*school*			
español	*Spanish*			
estado (m)	*state, condition*			
están	*(they) are | are being | (you (pl formal)) are | are being*			
estricto	*strict*			
estudiante (mf)	*student*			
estudiar	*(to) study | studying*			
estudio (m)	*study*			
examen (m)	*exam*			
excelente	*excellent*			
exposición (f)	*exhibition, display*			

falda (f)	*skirt*			
faltar	*(to) be missing, lack | being missing, lacking*			
fecha (f)	*date*			
formación (f)	*training, education*			
gastar	*(to) spend (money) | spending (money)*			
gran	*big, great (m, f) (pre-noun)*			
gris	*grey, gloomy*			
gritar	*(to) shout | shouting*			
habría	*there would be*			
hacia	*toward, towards*			
haría	*(I) would do, make*			
historia (f)	*history, story*			
horario (m)	*timetable, schedule*			
humor (m)	*humour*			
importancia (f)	*importance, significance*			
imposible	*impossible*			
incluso	*including, even*			
independiente	*independent*			
instalaciones (fpl)	*facilities*			
instituto (m)	*school, high school, institute*			
jamás	*never*			
jersey (m)	*jumper*			
jueves (m)	*Thursday*			
lago (m)	*lake*			
llevar; **llevar + time period + present participle**; llevarse (con)	*(to) wear, carry, take, lead | wearing, carrying, taking, leading;* ***(to) have been + -ing + for + time****; (to) get on (with) | getting on (with)*			
lugar (m)	*place*			
lunes (m)	*Monday*			

		😕	🙂	😎
mantener; mantenerse	*(to) maintain, keep / maintaining, keeping; to keep, stay / keeping, staying*			
maravilloso	*marvellous, wonderful*			
martes (m)	*Tuesday*			
matemáticas (fpl)	*Maths*			
memoria (f)	*memory*			
menos	*except, minus*			
miedo (m)	*fear*			
momento (m)	*moment*			
nacional	*national*			
ningún	*no, not...any (m, before a noun)*			
ninguno	*no, not...any (m)*			
ninguno, (no) ninguno	*no-one, none, (a single) one (after negative verb), anyone (after negative verb)*			
nivel (m)	*level*			
norma (f)	*rule*			
número (m)	*number, shoe size*			
obra (f)	*play*			
ofrecer	*(to) offer / offering*			
olvidar	*(to) forget / forgetting*			
orquesta (f)	*orchestra, dance band*			
oscuro	*dark*			
pantalones (mpl)	*trousers*			
patio (m)	*playground, courtyard*			
perder; perderse	*(to) lose, waste, miss / losing, wasting, missing; (to) get lost / getting lost*			
perfectamente	*perfectly*			
perfecto	*perfect*			

		😕	🙂	😎
permitir	*(to) allow / allowing*			
personal	*personal*			
pesado	*heavy, boring, annoying*			
pintar	*(to) paint / painting*			
poco	*a few, not much, not many*			
podría	*(I) would be able to*			
pondría; me pondría	*I would put; (I) would put (on), get, become*			
práctico	*practical, convenient*			
precio (m)	*price*			
pregunta (f)	*question*			
preguntar	*(to) ask / asking*			
presente (m)	*present*			
profesional	*professional*			
profesor (m), profesora (f)	*teacher, professor*			
prueba (f)	*class test*			
querría	*(I) would want, love*			
radio (f)	*radio*			
rápidamente	*quickly*			
real	*real, royal*			
realmente	*really*			
reciente	*recent*			
recientemente	*recently*			
recordar	*(to) remember, remind / remembering, reminding*			
reducir	*(to) reduce / reducing*			
regla (f)	*ruler, rule, regulation*			
religión (f)	*religion*			
repetir	*(to) repeat / repeating*			
resolver	*(to) solve, resolve / solving, resolving*			

respeto (m)	*respect*
sabría	*(I) would know (how to)*
sacar buenas / malas notas	*to get good/bad grades*
saldría	*(I) would go out, leave*
se me da bien/mal (el español)	*I am good/bad at (Spanish)*
segundo	*second*
segundo (m)	*second (time measurement)*
seguramente	*surely, certainly*
señora	*Mrs, lady, madam*
sentado	*sitting, seated*
sentido (m)	*sense, direction*
septiembre	*September*
serio	*serious*
servir	*(to) serve / serving*
silencio (m)	*silence*
simplemente	*simply*
solamente	*only*
sólo	*only, just*
sonrisa (f)	*smile*
sufrir	*(to) suffer, be in pain / suffering, being in pain*
superior	*superior, higher, upper*
tarea (f)	*task, job, homework, chore*
teatro (m)	*theatre*
tecnología (f)	*technology*
teléfono (m)	*(tele)phone*
temperatura (f)	*temperature*
tendría; tendría que	*(I) would have; would have to*
tercer	*third (m) (pre-noun)*
tercero	*third*
terminar(se)	*(to) finish, end / finishing, ending*
texto (m)	*text*
tocar	*(to) play (instrument), touch / playing (instrument), touching*
trabajador	*hardworking*
trabajadora	*hardworking*
trabajar	*(to) work / working*
tratar(se); tratar de + inf. (to)	*(to) treat, be about / treating, being about; try to (+ verb) / trying to (+ verb)*
uniforme (m)	*uniform*
urbano	*urban*
vendría	*(I) would come*
verdaderamente	*truly*
vestido (m)	*dress*
ya que	*since*
zapatillas de deporte (fpl)	*trainers*
zapato (m)	*shoe*

Foundation translation revision

Spanish to English

1 Use the English sentences to help you complete the Spanish translations.

1 Mis clases comienzan a las nueve menos cuarto y terminan a las tres y media.

My lessons .... at quarter to .... and finish at three ....

2 Estoy enfermo y me duele mucho la garganta desde hace tres días.

I am .... and my .... has been hurting for three ....

3 El último día hice un viaje en barco y vi unas vistas increíbles.

The last day .... on a trip by .... and I saw some incredible ....

4 Quedamos a la seis en la biblioteca y después podemos ir al club de dibujo.

Let's .... at six in the .... and then we can go to .... club.

5 Ayer perdí mi móvil en el metro y ahora no puedo subir vídeos o mandar mensajes.

Yesterday .... my phone on the underground and now I can't .... videos or .... messages.

2 Circle the two deliberate errors in each English translation.

1 De vez en cuando disfrutamos de escuchar canciones cuando hacemos deporte.

From time to time I enjoy listening to a song when we do sport.

2 En invierno cojo el autobús porque es más seguro que ir a pie .

During summer I catch the bus because it is more practical than going on foot.

3 Siempre me divierto mucho con mi mejor amiga porque me hace reír.

I sometimes have lots of fun with my best friend because he makes me laugh.

4 Cuando era más joven, me levantaba tarde porque no tenía mucha energía.

When I was younger, I went to bed late because I had lots of energy.

3 Underline the Spanish parts in this tangled text. Then rewrite the whole text in English on a separate sheet.

Mis padres say that I am muy trabajador y bastante responsable. I think that mi mejor amiga is always simpática y we have mucho en común. Also hacemos muchas cosas juntas and we never discutimos. En el instituto my friend and I siempre llegamos temprano y queremos to get buenas notas.

4 Translate these sentences into English on a separate sheet.

1 Para el almuerzo tomo un bocadillo.

2 Después del instituto tocamos en una banda.

3 Cuando llueve, quedamos en el centro comercial.

4 Cuando era más joven, no hacía mucho deporte en mi escuela.

What tense is this? How will you translate this phrase?

5 Para sacar buenas notas, voy a divertirme menos en clase.

English to Spanish

1 Read the paragraph in English. Number the boxes next to the Spanish sentences to put them in the correct order.

A week ago I watched a series with my best friend. Next week we are going to go to the cinema to see an adventure film. My best friend accepts me as I am and always listens to me. The things that interest him are education and family. The subjects that I like the most are very useful like technology.

Mi mejor amigo me acepta como soy y siempre me escucha. ☐

Las asignaturas que más me gustan son muy útiles, como la tecnología. ☐

Hace una semana vi una serie con mi mejor amigo. ☐

Las cosas que le interesan son la educación y la familia. ☐

La próxima semana vamos a ir al cine para ver una película de aventura. ☐

2 Translate these sentences into Spanish on a separate sheet, using the words from the grid.

1 I never do a show at school.

2 Yesterday I watched a match with my girlfriend.

3 Every day I used to eat fast food in the square.

4 From time to time they fight for a better world.

5 Two days ago I went to the cinema before going to sleep.

Ayer	comía	al cine	antes de dormir
De vez en cuando	fui	comida rápida	con mi novia
Hace dos días	luchan	por un mundo mejor	en el colegio
Nunca	participo en	un espectáculo	en la plaza
Todos los días	vi	un partido	

3 Use the English sentences to help you complete the Spanish translations.

1 When it is sunny, you can enjoy shows. *Cuando hace sol,* ....

2 My dream is to fight for a better planet. *Mi sueño es* ....

3 Social media is bad for mental health. *Las redes sociales* ....

4 Since yesterday my head has been hurting. *Desde ayer* ....

5 If I do more sport, I will sleep better. *Si practico* ....

4 Translate these sentences into Spanish on a separate sheet.

1 For dinner I have fish.

2 My dream is to be successful.

This is translated by a phrase using *tener*.

3 She never catches the train because it is expensive.

4 From time to time I have fun with my aunt and uncle.

Think about how you translate plurals of family members.

5 Two weeks ago I stopped eating fast food.

Use the verb expression *dejar de* in the correct tense.

Higher translation revision

Spanish to English

1 Read the email and translate the words below into English.

El año pasado me quedé en un camping agradable en la costa con mi familia. Desafortunadamente, no había piscina y hacía mucho calor. El último día me caí en la playa y me rompí el dedo. ¡Fue terrible! Tuvimos que ir al médico inmediatamente.

1 me quedé ....
2 agradable ....
3 desafortunadamente ....
4 no había ....
5 me caí ....
6 el dedo ....
7 fue ....
8 tuvimos que ....

2 Read the text and tick the three correctly translated sentences in English.

Cuando era más pequeño, no me levantaba temprano y siempre llegaba tarde al instituto. Muchas veces olvidaba algo importante, como mi bolígrafo o mi cuaderno y nunca escuchaba al profesor. Ahora tengo una actitud más positiva y hago todas las tareas.

1 When I was smaller, I used to get up early but I would always arrive at school late. ☐
2 When I was smaller, I didn't use to get up early and I would always arrive at school late. ☐
3 Many times I used to forget something important, like my pen or my exercise book. ☐
4 Many times I used to forget something, like my ruler or my exercise book. ☐
5 I have a better attitude now and I do most tasks. ☐
6 I have a more positive attitude now and I do all tasks. ☐

3 Use the English sentences to help you complete the Spanish translations.

1 La ciudad era muy hermosa, pero hizo mucho viento el tercer día.

The city was very ....

2 En mi instituto cambiaría los edificios porque son bastante viejos.

In my school I ....

3 Si te interesa el baile, hay que participar en la fiesta cultural.

If you are interested in ....

4 Esta tarde ponen una película buena, pero termina muy tarde.

This afternoon they ....

5 Creo que viajar en avión es mejor porque puedes leer revistas y ver películas.

I think that travelling ....

4 Translate this paragraph into English on a separate sheet.

Estoy triste porque no me llevo bien con mi madre. Nunca me apoya y es seria. Ayer discutimos porque dejé mi móvil en el autobús cuando volví del instituto. Siempre se queja si paso demasiadas horas delante de una pantalla y ahora está enfadada porque estoy jugando al fútbol. No sé cómo llevarme mejor con ella.

English to Spanish

1 Use the word mosaic to translate each sentence into Spanish on a separate sheet. You can use words more than once.

1 Social media can be dangerous and many users argue.

2 Many young people prefer watching series and posting images.

3 You can see dangerous images and meet followers.

4 I usually watch the news on TV, but many young people prefer social media.

5 Many young users prefer social media, but I usually watch the TV.

las redes	suelo	sociales	conocer a	para	colgar
la tele	series	pueden	en	discuten	las noticias
seguidores	se	jóvenes	y	imágenes	ser
pero	ver	muchos	peligrosas	usuarios	prefieren

2 Underline the English parts in this tangled text. Then rewrite the whole text in Spanish underneath.

I have una dieta sana e intento eat well. Todos los días I go to bed temprano y normalmente I have breakfast at the misma hora, después de doing exercise. While hago los deberes, siempre I drink a lot of water and I eat fruta. I try to avoid comer cakes o bebidas with too much sugar.

....

....

....

....

3 Translate this paragraph into Spanish.

I have quite a healthy diet because I am vegan. My lunch consists of a plate of vegetables with rice. To have a healthy diet at school is quite difficult because you have to be careful with the amount of unhealthy food you eat. For example, after orchestra club last week, I ate a big afternoon snack with lots of sugar. Next week we are going to bring fruit.

Translate this using one word.

Remember that 'to be careful' is translated using an expression with *tener*.

....

....

....

....

Zona de cultura
En Colombia todo es posible

F Talking about your area (revising adjectival agreement)

1 Write the correct letter to match up the places with the descriptions.

1 Hay una playa blanca y el mar tiene una temperatura agradable. ☐
2 Aquí se puede hacer deporte y en invierno nieva mucho. ☐
3 Allí vive mucha gente y hay muchas tiendas, y bibliotecas. ☐
4 Su capital es grande y tiene varias ciudades históricas, muchas costas increíbles y montañas altas. ☐

a Es un país en Latinoamérica.
b Son unas montañas bonitas.
c Es una ciudad interesante.
d Es una costa bella.

G

Remember to make **adjectives** agree with the nouns they describe. Some adjectives only change in the plural but those ending in ***-o*** have four different endings.

Pay attention to number and gender when writing the articles (the, a, some) before nouns.

un país increíble	an incredible country	*unos platos rico**s***	some tasty dishes
*un**a** provincia bell**a***	a beautiful province	*el puerto modern**o***	the modern port
*un**as** playas blanc**as***	some white beaches	*las flores bell**as***	the beautiful flowers

2 Complete each phrase with the correct adjective from the box, paying attention to the endings.

bello, histórico, tranquilo, perfecto, increíble, agradable, grande

1 Creo que mi región, en el oeste, es muy .... (*calm*)
2 En el norte tenemos unos pueblos .... (*historic*)
3 En el sur hay una ciudad .... (*perfect*)
4 No hay playas .... (*beautiful*) en el este, pero hay un clima .... (*nice*)
5 En la provincia central tenemos muchas montañas .... (*big*) y vistas .... (*incredible*)

3 Translate these sentences into Spanish.

1 I live in a beautiful region. ....
2 My province has big beaches. ....
3 In the north there are some incredible woods. ....
4 A historic town is located in the west. ....

Translate this using the phrase *se encuentra*.

5 We went to a nice coast because it is a great destination in summer.

....

Zona de cultura
En Colombia todo es posible

H Recognising demonstrative adjectives

H 1 Tick the correct box to choose the correct translation for each sentence.

1 Esta región verde tiene unos árboles hermosos.
  a This big region has a beautiful tree. ☐
  b This green region has some beautiful trees. ☐
2 En este pueblo se encuentra un río pequeño.
  a A small lake is located in this city. ☐
  b A small river is located in this town. ☐
3 Este paisaje histórico es famoso en esta provincia.
  a This historic landscape is famous in this province. ☐
  b This historic country is famous for its provinces. ☐

G

H Demonstrative adjectives are used to translate 'this', 'that', 'these' and 'those'. The adjective comes before and agrees with the noun.

este paisaje	*esta carretera*
ese bosque	*esa esquina*
estos pájaros	*estas calles*
esos lagos	*esas regiones*

H 2 Circle the correct article and adjective to complete each sentence.

1 Es verdad que tenemos **muchas** / **muchos** especies de pájaros en este bosque y **un** / **una** clima **húmedo** / **húmeda**.
2 Mi provincia posee **varios** / **varias** paisajes con **esas** / **esos** árboles famosos que ves en la tele.
3 **Esta** / **Este** región es **reconocido** / **reconocida** en el mundo como **uno** / **una** de los lugares más bellos de Latinoamérica.
4 **Estos** / **Estas** lagos **enormes** / **enorme** se encuentran en el oeste del país, donde hay **un** / **unas** plantas increíbles.

H 3 Underline the English parts in this tangled text. Then rewrite the whole text in Spanish.

This provincia has muchos landscapes especiales with a great variety of animales y flowers. It is found in the centre de mi país. Creo que my region has una gran quantity of árboles and birds. Es un hermoso destination para enjoy nature y de las playas de white sand.

....

....

....

....

H 4 Translate this paragraph into English on a separate sheet.

Soy colombiano y vivo en el sur. En mi país los habitantes son muy agradables. El país tiene muchas provincias con una gran variedad de naturaleza y animales. En mi región hay una ciudad que tiene un río amplio y muy hermoso en el centro. Cerca del río hay una fila de casas pintadas de varios colores.

This adjective is formed from the verb *pintar*. Can you remember what it means? It was used in Module 5.

1 Medellín, ciudad inteligente

Using the perfect tense

1 Draw lines to match up the sentence halves.

1 He viajado
2 Nosotras hemos visto mucho
3 Mi amigo ha bebido
4 Mis padres han aprendido
5 Hemos visitado

a unos monumentos históricos.
b en metro en mi barrio.
c un café en el centro comercial.
d arte en las calles.
e mucho sobre la historia en el museo.

2 Complete each sentence with the correct preposition of place from the box. Remember to include the article for the noun that comes after: *del, de la, de los, de las*.

a través de | al lado de | cerca de | delante de | detrás de | lejos de

1 Hemos visitado el castillo que está .... (*behind*) museo.
2 He visto el palacio que está .... (*next to*) oficina de correos.
3 He comprado unos recuerdos en la tienda que está .... (*near to*) plaza.
H 4 El puente ha cambiado mucho .... (*through*) siglos.

G

Use the **perfect tense** to talk about something you have done.
Use the present tense of ***haber*** **+ past participle**.

(yo) (tú) (él/ella/usted) (nosotros/as) (vosotros/as) (ellos/as/ustedes)	he has ha hemos habéis han	**cerrado** **comido** **subido**

3 Circle the correct form of *haber* to complete these sentences. Then translate each one into English.

1 Fátima y Lola **he** / **has** / **han** ido a Correos.

....

2 ¿Vosotras **hemos** / **has** / **habéis** visitado el palacio?

....

3 Nosotros **han** / **he** / **hemos** pasado el puente.

....

4 Yo **has** / **ha** / **he** aprendido mi nueva dirección.

....

Watch out for **false friends** when you are translating. For example, the word ***dirección*** does not mean 'direction' in this context. It means 'address'.

4 Complete these sentences by using the correct past participle form of the word in brackets.

1 Ya hemos .... (*viajar*) en tren en Medellín.

2 Mis padres todavía no han .... (*ver*) un pueblo típico.

3 La tienda cerca de mi casa ya ha .... (*abrir*).

H 4 Usted ha .... (*descubrir*) unos lugares maravillosos.

G There are some irregular past participles to learn.

abrir (to open)	→ ***abierto***
decir (to say)	→ ***dicho***
escribir (to write)	→ ***escrito***
hacer (to do/make)	→ ***hecho***
poner (to put)	→ ***puesto***
romper (to break)	→ ***roto***
ver (to see)	→ ***visto***
volver (to return)	→ ***vuelto***
H *descubrir* (to discover)	→ ***descubierto***

H 5 Translate these sentences in the perfect tense into English.

1 Hemos atravesado la plaza para ver la fuente.

....

2 Ustedes han mirado los monumentos históricos del pueblo.

....

3 La tienda de ropa en el centro comercial ha cerrado temprano.

....

4 Mi amigo ha observado que hay muchas casas bellas en las afueras de la ciudad.

....

5 Hay más zonas verdes. Es un signo de que la ciudad ha cambiado.

....

When working out words you don't recognise, think about other words that you know that could help. For example, ***a través de*** means 'through', so ***atravesar*** means 'to go through'.

F 6 Translate these sentences into English on a separate sheet.

1 Mi barrio es grande. Está lejos del centro.

2 La puerta de la tienda de ropa está abierta.

3 Si quiero comprar algo, hay un centro comercial allí.

How do you give directions in English?

4 Cruza la plaza para ir a Correos. Está a la izquierda.

5 Ya he pasado el puente, pero no he visto el castillo todavía.

H 7 Translate this paragraph into Spanish on a separate sheet.

This is the same word in Spanish as the word for a 'bank'.

I often visit the stadium in the suburbs. We sometimes rest on a bench in the park. My friends live far from the square but near the fountain. They have already travelled by bike to the palace near the police station. I have not yet seen the historic palace.

Use *la comisaría* to translate this.

2 Medellín ahora y antes

Using demonstrative adjectives for descriptions

1 Write the correct letter to match up the questions with the answers.

1 ¿Te gusta vivir en Medellín?

2 ¿Qué te gusta hacer allá?

3 ¿Cómo es tu ciudad ahora?

4 ¿Cómo era antes?

5 ¿Cómo es la red de transporte?

a Creo que es un sitio muy seguro con muchos espacios verdes.

b Acá es bastante moderno porque tenemos un nuevo metro.

c Era más peligrosa y muchas tiendas de mi barrio estaban cerradas.

d Me encanta ir al centro comercial y, si tengo tiempo, voy al cine.

e Sí, me gusta mucho porque es una ciudad increíble.

2 Complete each sentence with in the correct present or imperfect tense verbs from the box.

1 Ahora la ciudad .... muchos espacios verdes.

2 El barrio es grande y .... varios edificios modernos.

3 Antes .... una carretera pequeña, pero ahora .... muy grande.

4 En el pasado mi pueblo .... unos barrios muy sucios en el centro.

5 Ahora en mi zona .... más cafés, pero antes en mi barrio no .... piscina.

In Spain, it's more common to translate 'here' with ***aquí*** and 'there' with ***ahí*** or ***allí***. In Latin America it's more common to use ***acá*** and ***allá***, respectively. You will need to learn all these for your GCSE exam.

es	tiene	hay
era	tenía	había

G

Demonstrative adjectives agree with the noun they describe.

this → *est**e** castillo* (this castle) — *est**a** plaza* (this square)
these → *est**os** sitios* (these places) — *est**as** tiendas* (these shops)

that → *es**e** cine* (that cinema) — *es**a** calle* (that street)
those → *es**os** barrios* (those districts) — *es**as** ciudades* (those cities)

Esto and ***eso*** refer to 'this' or 'that' (thing) and are not used with a noun.

*¿Qué es **esto**?* — What is **this** (thing)?
*¡**Eso** fue maravilloso!* — **That** was wonderful!

3 Circle the correct demonstrative adjective or pronoun to complete the sentence.

1 En **este** / **estos** / **esta** espacios hay muchas flores.

2 Vamos a mirar dónde está la biblioteca en **ese** / **esa** / **eso** mapa.

3 **Esas** / **Esa** / **Esos** calles están muy limpias, **esta** / **esa** / **eso** es verdad.

H 4 En el pasado había más delitos en **esto** / **esta** / **este** barrio.

H 5 Ahora hay más arquitectura moderna en **esta** / **estas** / **esta** ciudades.

4 Complete the missing words in the parallel translations.

	1	Esta .... está muy limpia y es más	This room is very .... and .... bigger.
	2	Esos edificios son ...., pero .... calle está sucia.	.... buildings are modern, but this .... is dirty.
	3	En el pasado .... zona tenía más .... y una estación de	In the .... this .... had more shops and an underground ....
H	4	.... mi ciudad era más .... porque había .... violencia en las calles.	Before my city .... safer because there was less .... on the ....
H	5	Ahora .... barrio no es muy .... porque .... mucho tráfico.	Now this .... is not .... calm because it has lots of ....

G

Aquel is another demonstrative pronoun that describes something that is further away from the time or place where the person is. We translate this as 'that/those ... over there'.

aquel *castillo*	that castle over there	***aquella*** *carretera*	that road over there
aquellos *días*	those days	***aquellas*** *zonas*	those areas over there

Aquello on its own means 'that' referring to something abstract.
Aquello *fue muy difícil.* That (thing) was very difficult.

H 5 Write the correct demonstrative adjective in each sentence (*aquel, aquella, aquellos, aquellas*). Then translate each sentence into English on a separate sheet.

1 En .... tiempos las calles estaban más limpias que ahora.

2 .... fuente es tan bonita que muchos turistas quieren verlo.

3 Mi amigo vive en .... barrio, que es muy tranquilo por las noches.

4 .... ciudad ha cambiado mucho en los últimos años.

F 6 Translate these sentences into Spanish.

1 This neighbourhood is pretty. ....

2 Now the streets are calm. ....

3 This area has many green spaces near the library. ....

4 Those buildings are not very modern. ....

5 Before, this city used to be much cleaner. ....

Do you need to use *era* or *estaba*?

H 7 Translate this paragraph into English on a separate sheet.

Vivo en una ciudad grandísima. Pienso que ha cambiado mucho en los últimos diez años. Es un lugar interesante con mucha cultura y arte. En el pasado había varios problemas: había mucha violencia y se veían más drogas en las calles. Ahora hay tantas cosas divertidas que hacer acá. Me encanta subir por la calle antigua hacia aquel castillo.

Think carefully about the word order of this phrase.

3 ¡A comprar!

Revising direct object pronouns

1 Draw lines to match up the questions with the answers.

1 ¿En qué puedo servirle?	**a** Sí, prefiero esta camiseta negra en la talla grande. Voy a comprarla.
2 ¿Quiere usted algo diferente?	**b** Es cuarenta y dos euros.
3 ¿Le gusta el vestido?	**c** Hola. Compré esta camisa blanca, pero es demasiado pequeña. La quiero cambiar.
4 ¿Hay una oferta?	**d** Sí, me encanta el vestido porque es de buena calidad. Lo voy a comprar también.
5 ¿Cuánto es?	**e** No tenemos oferta, pero es un buen precio.

2 Complete each sentence using a word from the box.

bolsillos	ropa
comercial	siempre
segunda	mejores
faldas	barata
comprar	cómoda

1 Me encanta la ropa deportiva porque es muy ....

2 Prefiero ir al centro .... porque los precios son ....

3 Odio .... por Internet porque es difícil ver la calidad de la ....

4 Me gustan las .... con .... porque son muy prácticas.

5 .... compro la ropa de .... mano porque es .... y tiene un estilo original.

G

Direct object pronouns normally go before the verb, but they can also be attached to the end of the infinitive. They need to agree with the noun they replace.

*El sombrero no es muy cómodo. No **lo** voy a llevar. / No voy a llevar**lo**.*
*No me gustan los zapatos. **Los** voy a devolver. / Voy a devolver**los**.*
*Compré una falda rosa. **La** llevo todos los días.*
*Prefiero ir a las tiendas de marca. **Las** visito los sábados.*

3 Circle the correct direct object pronoun to complete each sentence.

1 Quiero comprar unos regalos. **Los** / **Las** / **La** voy a comprar en el centro comercial.

2 Me encanta ver los monumentos. **Las** / **Los** / **Lo** vi ayer.

3 La ropa de segunda mano es barata. **Las** / **Lo** / **La** compro en línea.

H **4** Compré un traje, pero es demasiado ajustado. **Lo** / **La** / **Los** voy a devolver.

H **5** Las tiendas de mi barrio son adecuadas, pero no **la** / **los** / **las** visito porque siempre hay colas.

4 Read the sentences and circle the two deliberate mistakes in each one. Then write out the corrections.

1 En la mayoría de los centros commerciales no hay ropa de segunda mana.

2 Probablemente la ropa cuesta menos en línea, perro a veces la calidad es malo.

3 *Compré unos zapatos, pero las voy a cambiar porque es demasiado pequeños.*

H 4 *Ayer en las rebajas compro un reloj, pero la quiero devolver.*

H 5 *Esos zapatos ya no está a la venta, pero la tienda tienen buenas ofertas.*

H 5 Circle the correct noun in brackets that has been replaced in the sentence by an object pronoun. Then translate each sentence into English.

1 Lo devolví ayer. (**traje** / **zapatos** / **falda**)

2 Se los di a mi hermano. (**pantalón** / **botas** / **relojes**)

3 Voy a llevarlo a una fiesta. (**camisa** / **tallas** / **conjunto**)

4 Las quiero cambiar. (**zapatos** / **camisetas** / **calcetines**)

F 6 Translate these sentences into English.

1 No me gusta ir a las tiendas.

2 Los precios en línea son mejores y constantes.

3 Las cosas que compro son baratas.

What does this mean when placed before days, months or years?

4 Hace dos días compré este sombrero blanco, pero lo odio.

5 Me gustaría comprar algo de buena calidad.

Translate this the same as you would the expression 'to buy'.

H 7 Translate this paragraph into Spanish.

Many young people go to the shopping centre. They enjoy the experience of buying things. On one hand they say that they prefer to try on clothes. They often buy them after school. On the other hand they don't like to queue. Some shops have reduced their prices a lot. However, buying online is practical.

4 ¿Dónde prefieres vivir?

F Making comparisons

1 Draw lines to match up the sentence halves.

1 Prefiero vivir en Medellín porque
2 No me gustan las ciudades porque tienen
3 El transporte público es más barato
4 Muchos pisos tienen menos espacio
5 En el campo no hay tantos kilómetros de

a que las casas grandes con jardines.
b que viajar en coche.
c hay más posibilidades de trabajo.
d carretera o tanta gente.
e más polución en el aire que los pueblos.

2 Complete the sentence with either *es* or *está*.

1 Mi casa .... en un pueblo pequeño en la montaña.
2 El parque .... muy cerca de mi piso.
3 Esta calle .... tan grande como esa carretera.
4 Mejoraría la red de transporte porque .... demasiado caro.
5 Mi provincia .... tranquila porque hay menos gente que en la zona del norte.

3 For each comparison, identify the tense used: write F if it is future, C for conditional or P for present. Then translate each sentence into English.

1 La ciudad tendrá menos zonas verdes que antes. ☐

....

2 Las playas están tan limpias como los mares. ☐

....

3 Mi zona estará más tranquila después de las fiestas. ☐

....

4 El centro comercial tendría más ropa barata que las tiendas pequeñas. ☐

....

G

There are several ways to compare and contrast:

más ... que ...	more ... than ...
menos ... que ...	less ... than ...
tan ... como ...	as ... as ...

Remember, you can use ***más/menos*** + ***que*** with nouns or adjectives.

*Mi barrio tiene **menos** tiendas **que** el centro.*
*Las calles están **más** limpias **que** las playas.*

4 Translate the sentences into Spanish on a separate sheet.

1 I love living in a city. (Use the infinitive.)
2 My neighbourhood is very clean.
3 Here the flats are as big as the houses. (Which comparative do you need to use here?)
4 I would improve the hospitals because they are dirty.
5 Last week we travelled twenty kilometres to the mountains.

4 ¿Dónde prefieres vivir?

H Using the present subjunctive with *cuando*

H 1 Complete each sentence with the correct missing word in brackets.

1 Lo bueno de vivir en el .... es que no hay mucho ruido y el tráfico no llena las carreteras. (*ciudad / campo*)

2 Lo malo de mi zona es que los vecinos en los pisos no se .... (*conoce / conocen*)

3 Lo mejor de mi pueblo es que .... más posibilidades de trabajo. (*hay / es*)

4 Evidentemente lo positivo de los alrededores es que .... menos tráfico y polución que el centro. (*tienen / tiene*)

5 En mi opinión, lo negativo de los barrios lejanos es que la red de transporte público es .... (*peor / mejor*)

G

H The **present subjunctive** is needed when using ***cuando*** with future plans. To form the present subjunctive, take the first person singular in the present tense (the 'I' form) and remove the **-o**. For **-*ar*** verbs add ***e*** and for **-*er*/-*ir*** verbs add ***a***.
Ser and ***ir*** are irregular:

ser → *sea, seas, sea*
ir → *vaya, vayas, vaya*

*Cuando **sea** mayor, tendré un perro.*
When **I am** older, I will have a dog.

Infinitive	Present tense (*yo*)	Present subjunctive (*yo, tú, él/ella/usted*)
tener	*tengo*	*tenga, tengas, tenga*
hacer	*hago*	*haga, hagas, haga*
venir	*vengo*	*venga, vengas, venga*

H 2 Draw lines to match sentence halves. Use the English translations to help you.

1 Cuando venga a la ciudad,
2 Cuando haga el examen,
3 Cuando seas mayor,
4 Cuando vayas a esa tienda,

a estaré muy nervioso.
b vivirás en el extranjero en una ciudad divertida.
c comprarás unos productos sostenibles.
d verá a aún más gente en las calles.

1 When she comes to the city, she will see even more people on the streets.
2 When I take the exam, I will be very nervous.
3 When you are older, you will live abroad in a fun city.
4 When you go to that shop, you will buy some sustainable products.

H 3 Complete each sentence with the correct present subjunctive form of the verb in brackets.

1 Cuando .... tiempo, leeré más libros porque me encanta la lectura. (*tener*)

2 Cuando .... mi amigo a casa, jugaremos con mi gato. (*venir*)

3 Cuando .... mayor, ¿dónde quieres vivir? (*ser*)

4 Cuando mi madre .... al centro, comprará ropa sostenible. (*ir*)

5 Cuando .... las compras, encontrarás más rebajas en las tiendas grandes. (*hacer*)

H 4 Translate this paragraph into English on a separate sheet.

What tense is this?

Vivimos en un barrio precioso. Lo bueno de mi ciudad es que está a cuarenta kilómetros de la costa. Lo malo es el transporte y por eso aumentaría el número de trenes por hora. Cuando vaya al centro, iré a la nueva tienda de ropa sostenible. Aún no he decidido qué comprar.

5 Un intercambio cultural

Using irregular preterite verbs and other tenses

1 Draw lines to match up the questions with the answers.

1 ¿Dónde vives?

2 ¿Cuál es tu sitio favorito de tu zona?

3 ¿Cómo es tu casa?

4 ¿Qué hiciste el fin de semana pasado?

5 ¿Qué harás este fin de semana?

a Hay varios sitios familiares que me encantan, como la plaza.

b Quiero ir a la playa a jugar al voleibol y disfrutar del aire puro.

c Es bastante grande. Arriba hay tres cuartos y abajo hay una cocina.

d Vivo en una casa en el centro de un pueblo pequeño.

e Participé en un evento musical en el parque que está cerca de mi casa.

G

Remember that some verbs are completely irregular in the **preterite tense**.

ir/ser → *fui, fuiste, fue, fuimos, fuisteis, fueron*
dar → *di, diste, dio, dimos, disteis, dieron*
traer → *traje, trajiste, trajo, trajimos, trajisteis, trajeron*

2 Read the English and unjumble the Spanish words to write the translation.

1 My boyfriend brought me a present. *trajo me novio regalo Mi un*

....

2 They went to the restaurant on the corner. *la restaurante al en esquina Fueron*

....

3 The girl threw a party at the weekend. *La fin una dio el semana chica fiesta de*

....

4 We gave souvenirs to our neighbours after the visit. *nuestros visita a recuerdos después de la dimos vecinos Les*

....

3 Identify the tense in each sentence: write P if it is preterite, Pr for present or F for future. Then translate each sentence into English.

1 Encontré tu móvil perdido encima de la mesa en tu cuarto – ¡de nada!

....

2 Pues, en mi opinión mis vecinos son muy agradables.

....

3 Habrá más eventos en la plaza después del concierto.

....

4 Fuimos a muchas tiendas y compramos unos recuerdos bonitos.

....

H 5 Vieron mucha alegría en las calles durante la excursión en autobús.

....

G

Other preterite verbs have irregular stems but mainly follow familiar patterns.

decir → *dije, dijiste, dijo, dijimos, dijisteis, dijeron*
hacer → *hice, hiciste, hi**z**o, hicimos, hicisteis, hicieron*
querer → *quise, quisiste, quiso, quisimos, quisisteis, quisieron*
venir → *vine, viniste, vino, vinimos, vinisteis, vinieron*
estar → *estuve, estuviste, estuvo, estuvimos, estuvisteis, estuvieron*
poder → *pude, pudiste, pudo, pudimos, pudisteis, pudieron*
poner → *puse, pusiste, puso, pusimos, pusisteis, pusieron*
saber → *supe, supiste, supo, supimos, supisteis, supieron*
tener → *tuve, tuviste, tuvo, tuvimos, tuvisteis, tuvieron*

4 Complete each gap with the correct word from the box.

quise	cuando	creer	evento
dimos	partes	pude	debajo

1 El domingo mi familia y yo .... una fiesta para celebrar un gran .... en el barrio.

2 .... ir a la playa, pero llovió mucho, así que no .... salir y me puse a descansar.

H 3 .... llegué al parque inmenso, me di cuenta de que mi pañuelo estaba .... de mi cama.

H 4 Por todas .... había muchas personas quienes hacían mucho ruido y no pude .... la cantidad de comida en la calle.

H 5 Complete the missing words in the parallel translations.

.... de mi edificio hay .... diez árboles. Es .... que mis vecinos quieren crear un .... hermoso. Por ejemplo, mi .... de arriba, la que es muy lista, prometió poner más .... allá. Van a .... y ser hermosas. Estoy .... porque la .... de tener un jardín mediano es increíble.

Around my ...., there are approximately ten .... It is obvious that my .... want to create a .... garden. For example, my neighbour from ...., the one who is very ...., promised to put more flowers there. They are going to grow and be .... I'm happy because the possibility of having a ....-sized garden is incredible.

H 6 Translate these sentences into English.

1 Mi piso es pequeño pero cómodo. ....

2 Arriba tenemos un cuarto moderno. ....

3 Mis vecinos tienen muchas flores en su jardín. ....

4 Ayer estuvimos cerca del palacio y compré un café. ....

5 La próxima vez iré al estadio para ver un partido. ....

H 7 Translate this paragraph into Spanish on a separate sheet.

Use *un plano.*

In the town centre there are lots of things to visit. For example, you can follow the signs to the library or the castle. Yesterday we went to a park and my friend gave me a map. It is worth bringing a map because it is immense. We did so much there. I imagine that we will go back soon.

Use the expression which starts with these letters: v___ l_ p___.

Glossary

bold = this word will appear in Higher exams only

abajo	*downstairs, down, below*			
abierto	*opened*			
abierto	*open*			
acá	*here*			
adecuado	*appropriate, adequate*			
afueras (fpl)	*suburb, outskirts*			
agradable	*nice, pleasant*			
ahí	*there*			
ahora	*now*			
aire (m)	*air*			
ajustado	*tight*			
al lado (de)	*next to*			
alegría (f)	*joy, happiness*			
allá	*there*			
allí	*there, over there*			
alrededor (de)	*around, approximately*			
alrededores (mpl)	*surrounding area, vicinity*			
aproximadamente	*approximately*			
aquel, aquella	*that (m, f)*			
aquellos, aquellas	*those (m, f)*			
aquello	*that (thing)*			
aquí	*here*			
arquitectura (f)	*architecture*			
arriba	*upstairs, up there*			
atravesar	*(to) cross | crossing*			
aún	*still, yet*			
banco (m)	*bank, bench*			
barrio (m)	*neighbourhood, district*			
bello	*beautiful*			
bolsillo (m)	*pocket*			
bosque (m)	*wood, forest*			
calidad (f)	*quality*			
calle (f)	*street, road*			
capital (f)	*capital city*			
carretera (f)	*main road*			
casa (f)	*house*			
castillo (m)	*castle*			
central	*central*			
centro comercial (m)	*shopping centre*			
cerrado	*closed, closed-minded*			
cerrar	*(to) close, shut | closing, shutting*			
ciudad (f)	*city*			
cola (f)	*queue, glue*			
colombiano	*Colombian*			
comisaría (f)	*police station*			
conjunto (m)	*outfit*			
constante	*constant*			
correos (m), oficina de correos (f)	*post office*			
costar	*(to) cost | costing*			
crecer	*(to) grow up | growing up*			
cruzar	*(to) cross | crossing*			
de nada	*you are welcome, not at all*			
debajo (de)	*underneath | below, under*			
delito (m)	*crime, offense*			
descubierto	*discovered (past participle)*			
detrás (de)	*behind, at the back*			
devolver	*(to) give back, return | giving back, returning*			
dicho	*said, told*			

		😐	🙂	😎
dije	*(I) said, told*			
dimos	*(we) gave*			
dio	*(she, he, it, one) gave / (you (sing formal)) gave*			
dirección (f)	*address, direction*			
diste	*(you (sing informal)) gave*			
disteis	*(you (pl informal)) gave*			
droga (f)	*drug*			
ejemplo (m)	*example*			
el que, la que, los que, las que	*that/those, which, who (m, f, mpl, fpl) (subj)*			
encima (de)	*above*			
esa	*that (f)*			
escrito	*written*			
ese	*that (m)*			
eso	*that (thing)*			
esos, esas	*those (m) (f)*			
espacio (m)	*space*			
especie (f)	*species, kind*			
esquina (f)	*corner*			
esta	*this (f)*			
este	*this (m)*			
este (m)	*East*			
estilo (m)	*style, elegance, manner*			
estos, estas	*these (m) (f)*			
estuve	*(I) was*			
euro (m)	*Euro*			
evento (m)	*event*			
evidente	*obvious*			
evidentemente	*evidently, obviously*			
excursión (f)	*outing, trip*			
familiar	*familiar, of the family, family-sized*			
fila (f)	*line, row*			
flor (f)	*flower*			
fuente (f)	*fountain*			
gato (m)	*cat*			
ha...	*(she, he, it, one) has (+pp) / (you (sing formal)) have (+pp)*			
habéis...	*(you (pl informal)) have (+pp)*			
haber	*(to) have (done something)*			
habitante (mf)	*inhabitant*			
haga	*(I) do, make (subjunctive) / (she, he, it, one) does, makes (subjunctive) / (you (sing formal)) do, make (subjunctive)*			
hagas	*(you (sing informal)) do, make (subjunctive)*			
han...	*(they) have (+pp) / (you (pl formal) have (+pp)*			
has...	*(you (sing informal)) have (+pp)*			
he...	*(I) have (+pp)*			
hecho	*done, made*			
hemos...	*(we) have (+pp)*			
histórico	*historic*			
hola	*hello, hi*			
húmedo	*wet, humid*			
imaginar(se)	*(to) imagine / imagining*			
inmenso	*inmense, huge, great*			
intercambio (m)	*exchange*			
kilómetro (m)	*kilometer*			
las	*them (f) (obj)*			
lectura (f)	*reading*			

lejano	*distant*			
lejos (de)	*far (away, off)*			
les	*(to) them (m, f) (indirect obj)*			
listo	*ready, clever*			
llenar	*(to) fill, fulfil | filling, fulfilling*			
lo	*him, it (m) (obj)*			
los	*the (mpl)*			
los	*them (m) (obj)*			
mapa (m)	*map*			
marca (f)	*brand, mark*			
más; más (...que)	*more; adj + -er (...than), more (...than)*			
mayoría (f)	*majority*			
Medellín (m)	*Medellin*			
mediano	*medium-sized*			
metro (m)	*metre, metro, underground*			
mirar	*(to) look, watch | looking, watching*			
montaña (f)	*mountain*			
monumento (m)	*monument*			
museo (m)	*museum*			
naturaleza (f)	*nature*			
nervioso	*nervous, anxious*			
norte (m)	*North*			
nosotras | **(a) nosotras**	*we (f) (subj) |* ***(to) us (emph)***			
nosotros | **(a) nosotros**	*we (m, mixed gender) (subj) |* ***(to) us (emph)***			
observar	*(to) observe, watch | observing, watching*			
oeste (m)	*West*			
oferta (f)	*offer*			
paisaje (m)	*landscape*			
pájaro (m)	*bird*			
palacio (m)	*palace*			
pañuelo (m)	*headscarf*			
perdido	*lost*			
piso (m)	*flat, apartment, floor*			
plano (m)	*map*			
planta (f)	*plant, floor*			
plaza (f)	*square, place, vacancy*			
por otro lado	*on the other hand*			
por todas partes	*everywhere*			
por un lado	*on one hand*			
poseer	*(to) own, possess | owning, possessing*			
posibilidad (f)	*possibility*			
precioso	*beautiful*			
probablemente	*probably, likely*			
prometer	*(to) promise | promising*			
provincia (f)	*province*			
pude	*(I) was able to, could*			
pueblo (m)	*village, town*			
puente (m)	*bridge*			
puerta (f)	*door*			
pues	*so, well, well then*			
puesto	*put*			
puro	*pure, clean*			
puse; me puse	*(I) put; I put (on), got, became*			
quien	*who, whom*			
quise	*(I) wanted, loved*			
rebajas (fpl)	*sales*			
regalo (m)	*present, gift*			
región (f)	*region*			
reloj (m)	*watch, clock*			
río (m)	*river*			
ropa (f)	*clothes*			
rosa	*pink*			

sala (f)	*room, hall*			
seas	*(you (sing informal)) are (subjunctive)*			
seguro	*sure, safe, secure*			
signo (m)	*sign*			
sitio (m)	*place, site*			
sobre	*on, on top of, about*			
sombrero (m)	*hat*			
sostenible	*sustainable*			
subir	*(to) get on (mode of transport), go up, upload, turn up (music) I getting on, going up, uploading, turning up*			
sur (m)	*south*			
talla (f)	*size of clothing*			
tanto	*so much*			
tienda (f)	*shop, tent*			
todavía, no... todavía, todavía no....	*still; not ... yet*			
tráfico (m)	*traffic*			
traje	*(I) brought*			
traje (m)	*suit, costume*			
tranquilo	*calm, tranquil, relaxed*			
través, a través de	*through, across*			
tú	*you (sing informal) (subj)*			
unos	*some (mpl)*			
usted / **(a) usted**	*you (sing formal) (subj) / (to) you (sing formal)*			
ustedes / **(a) ustedes**	*you (pl formal) (subj) / (to) you (pl formal)*			
valer	*(to) cost, be worth / costing, being worth*			
varios	*several*			
vayas; te vayas (de)	*(you (sing informal)) go (subjunctive); (you (sing informal)) leave (subjunctive)*			
vecino (m), vecina (f)	*neighbour*			
venga	*(I) come (subjunctive) / (she, he, it, one) comes (subjunctive) / (you (sing formal)) come (subjunctive)*			
vengas	*(you (sing informal)) come (subjunctive)*			
venta (f)	*sale*			
verde	*green*			
vine	*(I) came*			
violencia (f)	*violence*			
visita (f)	*visit, guest at home*			
visto	*seen, watched*			
vosotras / **(a) vosotras**	*you (f) (pl informal) (subj) / (to) you (f) (pl informal) (emph)*			
vosotros / **(a) vosotros**	*you (m, mixed gender) (pl informal) (subj) / (to) you (m, mixed gender) (pl informal) (emph)*			
vuelto	*returned*			
ya	*already*			
zona (f)	*area, zone*			

Zona de cultura Espacios naturales maravillosos

- Using verbs of opinion
- **H** Using pronouns after prepositions

1 Complete each sentence using a word from the box. There are more words than gaps.

causa	montaña
colegio	pueblos
lejos	universidad
proteger	vuelve
cerca	dar

1 Me gusta estar al aire libre para estar .... de la naturaleza.

2 La polución .... problemas para todos.

3 Creo que es esencial luchar para .... el medio ambiente.

4 El cambio en el clima es extraordinario: hay menos nieve en la .... en invierno.

5 Reciclamos en casa y en el .... porque es la responsabilidad de todos.

2 Draw lines to match up the questions with the answers.

1 ¿Qué te importa hoy en día?

2 ¿Cómo es el río?

3 ¿Qué te gusta más de esta región?

4 ¿Qué haces para ayudar el medio ambiente?

5 ¿Qué reciclaste la semana pasada?

6 ¿Cómo era esta región en el pasado?

a Es largo, azul y muy bonito.

b Reciclé papel y plástico.

c Compro ropa de segunda mano.

d Me importa el medio ambiente.

e Era más verde y había más agua.

f La cosa que más me gusta son las montañas.

3 Complete the paragraphs using the words in the box.

encantaría interesa interesan pienso quiero

.... visitar un país con montañas. Las estudié en el colegio. .... que son bonitas, pero me interesan menos que los bosques.

Lola

Cris

Pienso que la naturaleza es increíble, sobre todo los bosques. Cambian en cada momento del año y hay muchos animales que viven allí. Me .... mucho estudiarlos.

Me .... mucho los animales que viven en el mar. Me .... verlos más de cerca cuando visito la costa.

Malek

4 Rewrite each sentence, putting the words into the correct order.

1 recursos Es naturales de tierra la esencial proteger los

....

2 gustaría Este ayuda año me asociación dar a local una

....

3 botellas En papel queremos reciclar de plástico casa y

....

4 educativo sobre Es aprender que problemas los nos día hoy en afectan

....

H 5 interesa mí luchar A me solo para no sino los peligro animales proteger a todos a en

....

Some phrases are already grouped together to help you.

H 6 difícil El algunas comportamiento de es de entender personas porque para ninguna ellos emergencia no hay

....

H 5 Complete these sentences with the correct preposition and pronoun.

Example: Nuestro jefe es buena persona. Podemos depender de él.

1 ...., el cambio climático es algo terrible. Vamos a participar en una manifestación. *(for us)*

2 El agua es muy importante. ...., los seres humanos no podrían sobrevivir. *(without it)*

3 ...., ¿cuál es el problema que más te interesa? *(to you)*

4 La energía renovable nos ayuda mucho. Gracias ...., hemos podido reducir la polución. *(to it)*

5 Los jóvenes se preocupan mucho por el medio ambiente. Tenemos que confiar .... para encontrar una solución. *(in them)*

G

H Prepositional pronouns are used after prepositions such as ***a***, ***de***, ***en***, ***para*** and ***sin***. Remember there is an accent on ***mí*** and ***él***, but not on ***ti***.
There are two irregular forms with ***con*** – ***conmigo*** (with me) and ***contigo*** (with you).

singular		plural	
me	***mí***	us	***nosotros/as***
you	***ti***	you	***vosotros/as***
him	***él***	them (masc)	***ellos***
her	***ella***	them (fem)	***ellas***
you (formal)	***usted***	you (formal)	***ustedes***

Use ***a*** + ***pronoun*** for emphasis.
*¿No te gusta el café? – ¡**A mí** me encanta!*

F 6 Translate these sentences into Spanish.

1 I want to be fit. ....

2 I like to ride my bike. ....

3 I go to the market to do the shopping. ....

4 It is important to walk or exercise every day.

....

5 Yesterday I tried to run to improve my health.

....

H 7 Translate this paragraph into English on a separate sheet.

A mí me importa el reciclaje. Creo que se debe prohibir el uso del plástico. Mi hermano se manifestó contra las causas de la crisis climática actual. El gobierno no se da cuenta de lo grave que es la situación. Quiero hacer una campaña para anunciar lo que podemos hacer en mi barrio.

1 ¡Actúa ya!

Using the imperative • Using the present and preterite tenses

G

Use the **imperative** to give instructions. For the singular (*tú*) positive imperative, remove the **-s** from the *tú* form of the present tense:

votar →	*(tú)* ***votas*** →	***¡Vota!***
proteger →	*(tú)* ***proteges*** →	***¡Protege!***
pedir →	*(tú)* ***pides*** →	***¡Pide!***

Remember that some verbs have an **irregular** form in the imperative:

decir (to say) →	*¡Di!*	***poner*** (to put) →	*¡Pon!*
hacer (to do, make) →	*¡Haz!*	***tener*** (to have) →	*¡Ten!*
ir (to go) →	*¡Ve!*	***venir*** (to come) →	*¡Ven!*
ser (to be) →	*¡Sé!*	***salir*** (to go out) →	*¡Sal!*

1 Draw lines to match up the Spanish commands with their English translations.

1 ¡Actúa ya!
2 ¡Haz algo para cambiar el mundo!
3 ¡Ayuda al medio ambiente!
4 ¡Lucha por una sociedad mejor!
5 ¡Limpia los parques y las playas!
6 ¡Publica tus ideas en las redes sociales!

a Fight for a better society!
b Clean up the parks and beaches!
c Help the environment!
d Do something to change the world!
e Post your ideas on social media!
f Act now!

2 Circle the correct verb to complete each sentence.

1 ¡**Di** / **Pide** algo para luchar por la gente pobre!
2 ¡**Sé** / **Habla** para mostrar tus propias opiniones!
3 ¡**Ve** / **Ten** una influencia positiva en tu comunidad!
4 ¡**Ven** / **Ten** a trabajar en un proyecto local!
5 ¡**Baja** / **Sube** tu uso de la energía!

G

Pronouns are added to the end of the **imperative**. Remember to add an accent to longer verbs to keep the stress in the right place

*¡Di**lo**!*	Say it!
*¡Ayúda**me**!*	Help me!

3 Change these sentences to use the imperative form of the verb and a pronoun.

Example: Tienes que pedir una sociedad igual para todos. *¡Pídela!*

1 Hay que respetar los derechos de las mujeres. ....
2 Tienes que ayudar a tu comunidad. ....
3 Tienes que proteger a los niños del racismo y del sexismo. ....
H 4 Hay que apoyar a las víctimas de violencia. ....
H 5 Hay que recoger la basura. ....
H 6 Tienes que prestar la ropa. ....

4 Complete each sentence using a verb from the box. There are more verbs than gaps.

1 Ayer mi amigo .... a trabajar en la caja de una asociación local.
2 Todos los días yo .... comida a las personas sin casa.
3 La semana pasada mi hermano .... la compra para unos ancianos.
4 Cada domingo él .... un evento para vender bolsas.
5 Hoy yo .... participar en un proyecto en mi barrio.
H 6 Actualmente nosotros estamos .... para defender los derechos de todos los ciudadanos.
H 7 Para ahorrar energía, ayer mis padres .... que apagar todas las luces en casa.

luchando
debí hizo
fue debo
di luchan
hace doy
fueron va
organiza
tuvieron
organizó

H 5 Draw lines to match up sentence halves. Think about the verb tenses.

1 A pesar de las dificultades en la sociedad, la gente
2 Después de las inundaciones, la isla
3 La lucha por la igualdad en la sociedad
4 Las personas con discapacidad
5 Si no actuamos, el cambio climático
6 A causa de la falta de trabajo, muchos jóvenes

a trae justicia para todos.
b va a destruir nuestro mundo.
c se recuperó cuando paró la lluvia.
d sigue votando por este gobierno.
e se fueron al extranjero.
f merecen tener acceso a todos los edificios.

F 6 Translate these sentences into English.

1 Trabajo en una asociación del barrio.

....

2 Participo en proyectos en mi comunidad.

....

3 Ayer pasé tiempo con mi vecina mayor.

....

4 Mi amiga vende ropa que no usa en línea.

....

5 Quiero mejorar la sociedad ayudando a otras personas.

....

H 7 Translate this paragraph into Spanish.

It is worthwhile being responsible and fair. It is necessary to help in your community. I take food to the homeless and clean the park in my area. My sister did a campaign to support an old people's home. I want to inform and give explanations about the problems that currently exist.

....

....

....

2 El planeta en peligro

Using the imperfect continuous tense • H Using the passive

1 Circle the correct verb to complete each sentence.

1 Cuando llueve en agosto, no **fui** / **voy** a la playa.

2 En 2024, **hizo** / **hace** mucho calor en el sur de España.

3 El clima está cambiando: **nevó** / **nieva** mucho menos ahora.

4 Hoy en día **hace** / **hizo** menos frío en las montañas.

5 Cuando me fui de vacaciones, no **llueve** / **llovió** y no había nubes en el cielo.

6 Ayer **hizo** / **hace** mucho viento al final.

2 Rewrite each sentence, putting the words into the correct order.

1 que problema es El altas principal hay más temperaturas

....

2 voz Hay el la para contra hablar clima cambio que usar del

....

3 en opiniones Tenemos las línea publicar que

....

4 algún La debería gente hacer comentario famosa

....

5 el Es adoptar actitud en futuro una positiva importante

....

H 6 falta comprar comercio Hace justo productos de

....

H 7 el y Basta con comportamiento actitudes las cambiar

....

3 Complete these sentences with the imperfect continuous form of the verb in brackets.

1 Yo .... a mi novio cuando llegó el autobús a la hora en punto. (*esperar*)

2 Tú .... el periódico en casa ayer por la mañana. (*leer*)

3 A las doce la mujer .... los servicios en la estación. (*limpiar*)

4 Yo .... cuando mis padres me dieron una sorpresa. (*comer*)

5 Por la tarde yo .... el resultado del partido en la radio. (*escuchar*)

H 6 Los niños se .... las clases cuando el profesor los vio. (*saltar*)

H 7 Nosotros .... al colegio cuando comenzó a nevar. (*andar*)

G

The **imperfect continuous** tense is used to describe what someone was doing. It is formed by using the imperfect tense of ***estar*** with the **present participle**:
*estaba compr**ando***
*estaba com**iendo***
*estaba sal**iendo***

H 4 Underline the English parts in this tangled text. Then rewrite the whole text in Spanish underneath.

Ayer, mientras que sus hermanos were repairing el coche, Marta was reading un artículo en un periódico británico. Una compañía inglesa was looking for jóvenes que wanted to formarse en tecnología en el Reino Unido durante el verano. Cuando su hermano mayor saw la expresión en la cara de Marta, él también began to read el artículo. Quizás su hermano could be mi aliado, pensó Marta. Al final él le dijo: "¡Vete a ask our parents! Es una oportunidad que no debes perder."

....

....

....

....

....

H 5 Complete the sentences with the passive form of the verb in brackets. Make sure you put it in the right tense.

1 La casa roja .... en 1950. (*construir*)

2 Los niños .... por sus padres. Están seguros. (*proteger*)

3 El año pasado el problema .... por la sequía. (*causar*)

4 El español .... en muchos de los países latinoamericanos. (*hablar*)

5 La bicicleta .... por mi madre ayer. (*comprar*)

6 Los edificios .... por el viento la semana pasada. (*destruir*)

7 El problema .... por los medios casi todos los días. (*mencionar*)

G

H The **passive** is used to say what is/was/will be done to something or someone. To form it, use the correct person and tense of ***ser*** followed by the past participle, which must agree.

*El artículo **fue** escrito en español.*

The article **was** written in Spanish.

F 6 Translate these sentences into Spanish.

1 I like to go to the beach. ....

2 It is nice weather in the summer. ....

3 Yesterday morning I was helping my mother. ....

4 I need to stop buying new clothes. ....

5 I want to fight against the changes in the climate. ....

H 7 Translate this paragraph into English on a separate sheet.

Creo que el planeta está en peligro actualmente. El tiempo está cambiando porque hace más calor y llueve más. No se debe esconder de las numerosas dificultades que hay. De hecho, recientemente mi familia y yo estábamos hablando de las consecuencias. Hace falta actuar y participar en el debate para tener un mundo mejor.

3 Protegemos el planeta

- Using three tenses in the 'I' and 'we' forms
- H Avoiding the passive

1 Complete each sentence using a word from the box. There are more words than gaps.

voy	compro
llevo	hago
pienso	reciclo
reduzco	pongo

1 .... ropa de segunda mano.
2 .... el papel, el plástico y los periódicos.
3 .... el uso del agua.
4 .... a pie o en bicicleta.
5 Siempre .... qué efecto mis acciones van a tener en mi comunidad.
6 .... una bolsa cuando voy de compras.

G

Use the **present tense** in the 'I' or 'we' forms to say what you usually do:
Uso/Usamos el transporte público.
Use the **preterite tense** in the 'I' or 'we' forms to say what you did in the past:
Estudié/Estudiamos el medio ambiente.
Use the **near future tense** in the 'I' or 'we' forms to say what you are going to do:
Voy/Vamos a reciclar más.

2 Draw lines to match up the sentence halves.

1 Mañana yo
2 El año pasado yo
3 Ayer mi hermano y yo
4 Normalmente yo
5 En el futuro nosotras

a ayudamos a limpiar el río.
b voy al colegio en bicicleta.
c vamos a usar el transporte público.
d voy a poner flores en el jardín.
e reciclé mucha ropa.

3 Rewrite each sentence, putting the words into the correct order.

1 cajas el y papel En reciclamos colegio

....

2 viajes hacer en En el voy futuro a más tren

....

3 el El paramos año de coche usar pasado

....

4 un protección por animales evento los Organicé para la de luchar

....

H 5 piscina Esta vamos el temporada a una en jardín meter

....

H 6 económico comida Comprar más local es

....

4 Complete the sentences with the correct form of the verb in brackets.

1 Ayer .... una presentación sobre el medio ambiente. (*I – hacer*)

2 Mis padres y yo .... a leer una publicación en Internet. (*we – ir*)

3 Ahora .... la suerte de vivir donde hay mucho transporte público. (*I – tener*)

4 Creo que siempre .... a llevar una bolsa al supermercado en el futuro. (*I – ir*)

5 .... el Día de la Tierra ayer. (*we – celebrar*)

H 6 No .... más el coche. No solo es malo para el planeta sino que así tampoco hago ejercicio. (*I – usar*)

H 7 .... a proponer una solución al problema del vidrio en la playa. (*we – ir*)

G

H You can avoid the passive by using the reflexive pronoun **se**.
Las normas ***se respetan***. *El evento* ***se celebró*** *ayer.*
Sometimes the subject follows the verb.
Se recicla *vidrio aquí.* *No* ***se escuchaba*** *la música.*

H 5 Rewrite each sentence using *se* to avoid the passive. There are two possible ways to do this for each sentence.

1 Su quinta novela fue publicada ayer.

....

2 Muchas campañas de reciclaje son hechas aquí.

....

3 Los alimentos son preparados en la cocina.

....

4 Muchos objetos son reciclados en nuestro pueblo.

....

5 El objetivo fue mencionado en la reunión.

....

F 6 Translate these sentences into English on a separate sheet.

1 Voy en bicicleta a menudo.

2 Es importante proteger el planeta.

3 Organizo muchos eventos en el barrio.

4 Ayer ayudé a limpiar el bosque en mi tiempo libre.

5 Mis amigos y yo queremos luchar de manera tranquila.

H 7 Translate this paragraph into Spanish on a separate sheet.

At our school, we separate the rubbish every week. Recycling events are often organised to have a positive effect. Last week I brought some materials for the campaigns. I would like to learn how to repair things and use them several times. We must all consider how to reduce the harm we do to the world.

4 Nuestro mundo, nuestra responsabilidad

- Using *(no) se debería* + infinitive
- H Using the subjunctive to give opinions

1 Draw lines to match up the problems with the solutions.

Use ***(no) se debería*** to say what you should (not) do. **G**

1 El río está muy sucio.
2 Muchas mujeres sufren violencia.
3 Usamos demasiada energía.
4 Hay mucho racismo en la sociedad.
5 Se usa mucha agua para hacer la ropa.
6 La comida es muy cara.

a Se debería respetar a todo el mundo.
b Se debería limpiar.
c No se debería comprar ropa nueva.
d No se debería tirar la comida.
e Se debería apagar el ordenador.
f No se debería aceptar la violencia.

2 Complete these sentences by translating the words in brackets. For each one, you will need the <u>infinitive</u>.

1 Creo que se debería .... (*protect*) el medio ambiente.
2 Los jóvenes deben .... (*have*) mucha influencia en el futuro del mundo.
3 Tenemos que .... (*improve*) la calidad del aire en las ciudades.
4 Hay que .... (*buy*) comida local.
5 Es necesario .... (*respect*) a todas las personas.
6 Nunca se debería .... (*forget*) la importancia de proteger nuestro planeta.

3 Complete each sentence using a word from the box.

comida interés minoría basura personaje racismo sociedad

1 En la serie el .... principal ayuda a cuidar el medio ambiente.
2 Hay mucha hambre en el mundo. Mucha gente no tiene suficiente .... Es una pena.
3 El sexismo y el .... son todavía verdaderos problemas.
4 Se debería intentar hacer una .... más segura para todos.
5 No se debería tirar .... en los parques.
H 6 El planeta siempre es un tema de .... para la juventud.
H 7 No obstante, hay una .... de gente que no nota los problemas.

4 Complete these sentences using *se debería* or *no se debería*.

1 .... hacer reciclaje.
2 .... dejar basura en el parque.
3 .... ayudar a la gente mayor en el barrio.
4 .... usar energía solo cuando se necesita.
5 .... ir siempre en coche.
6 .... olvidar a la gente sin casa en la sociedad.

H 7 .... limpiar el río seco para proteger a los peces.

H 8 .... bañar en condiciones peligrosas.

H The **present subjunctive** is used after verbs of wishing, command, request and emotion, like ***querer***, ***esperar***, ***recomendar*** and ***odiar***. Use it when there is a change of subject in the sentence. To form the present subjunctive, use the 'I' form of the present tense, take off the ***-o*** and add ***-e*** for ***-ar*** verbs and ***-a*** for ***-er*** and ***-ir*** verbs.
Irregular verbs include:
ser → *sea*
ir → *vaya*

G

H **5 Circle the correct form of the verb to complete the sentences.**

1 Recomiendo que te **compres** / **compras** un vehículo eléctrico.

2 Odio que mucha gente no **haga** / **hace** nada para ayudar a las personas con poco dinero.

3 Espero que él **tiene** / **tenga** su libertad pronto.

4 Mi madre me recomienda que **vaya** / **vayas** en tren.

5 Odio que ella **tengas** / **tenga** un vestido amarillo.

6 Mi novio quiere que el ambiente en el restaurante **es** / **sea** bueno.

F **6 Translate these sentences into Spanish.**

1 I spend time with an elderly neighbour.

....

2 I do the shopping for her at the market.

....

3 At the weekends, I clean up her garden.

....

4 Yesterday I went for a walk with Lola and her dog.

....

5 One should respect all the people in society.

....

H **7 Translate this paragraph into English.**

Me preocupa mucho el tema de la violencia. Muchas mujeres sufren debido al comportamiento de sus maridos. Tenemos que actuar a nivel mundial para cambiar las actitudes. Mis opiniones se basan en lo que leo sobre el sexismo en Internet. No me gusta que el hombre siempre tenga el poder en una relación.

....

....

....

....

5 El futuro está en nuestras manos

- Using the 'he/she/it' form in the present and the preterite
- H Using the relative pronoun *el cual*

G

When using the **preterite tense** in the 3rd person singular, remember to add an accent and stress the final syllable.

	-ar	**-er**	**-ir**
he/she/it	**-ó** *habló*	**-ió** *comió*	**-ió** *compartió*

Irregular verbs do not have a written accent and they have a normal stress pattern:

ir → *fue* ***ser*** → *fue* ***dar*** → *dio* ***tener*** → *tuvo*
poder → *pudo* ***hacer*** → *hizo* ***venir*** → *vino* ***estar*** → *estuvo*
querer → *quiso* ***decir*** → *dijo* ***traer*** → *trajo* ***poner*** → *puso*

1 Circle the correct preterite form to complete each sentence.

1 Mi hermano **puse** / **puso** / **pusiste** la caja bajo la mesa.

2 Tú **tuve** / **tuviste** / **tuvo** que limpiar la casa ayer.

3 Mi abuela **estuviste** / **estuve** / **estuvo** muy feliz cuando yo fui a visitarla.

4 Yo **compraste** / **compré** / **compró** otra versión del libro en línea.

5 Tu madre **salgo** / **salió** / **saliste** muy tarde esta mañana.

6 El profesor me **di** / **diste** / **dio** buenas notas ayer.

2 Rewrite each sentence, changing the verbs from the preterite to the present tense.

1 Mi actriz favorita puso un mensaje en una red social. Ayudó a unos niños que no tienen zapatos.

....

....

2 Mi jugador favorito dio dinero a personas sin casa. Escribió un blog para hablar del problema.

....

....

3 Mi cantante favorita participó en un evento para proteger el agua. Dijo que nunca se debería usar demasiada agua. ....

....

3 Complete these sentences using the present or preterite form of the verb in brackets.

1 El año pasado mi amigo .... en un proyecto para limpiar los bosques. (*participar*)

2 Después .... un blog sobre su trabajo. (*escribir*)

3 Más tarde lo .... en las redes sociales. (*publicar*)

4 Ahora .... trabajar para proteger a los animales que viven allí. (*intentar*)

5 Ayer me .... que está contento con todo lo que está haciendo. (*decir*)

H 6 Él no .... ver desaparecer una parte importante de la naturaleza. (*querer*)

H 7 El mes pasado .... un premio y ahora .... una figura conocida en la lucha universal para proteger los espacios verdes. (*ganar*, *ser*)

4 Decide if each sentence is written in the present (Pr), preterite (P) or future (F) tense and underline the verb(s).

1 Los niños escribieron algo sobre el tema del medio ambiente. ....

2 Mi hermano va a seguir una dieta vegetariana. ....

3 Yo estaba en el jardín cuando comenzó a llover. ....

4 No me pondré ropa de verano si hace frío mañana. ....

5 No debemos usar el coche para mejorar la calidad del aire en las ciudades. ....

H 6 Espero que la juventud haga más campañas para proteger las plantas. ....

H 7 Me molestó mucho el comportamiento de la gente que tiró basura en el parque. ....

H **5 Complete these sentences using the correct relative pronoun (*el cual, la cual, los cuales, las cuales*).**

1 El actor quiere hacer una obra, ... tendrá un mensaje positivo.

2 Hay que conservar el agua, ... es necesaria para vivir.

3 El sexismo y el racismo, ... no son legales, todavía producen problemas hoy en día.

4 El castillo, ... tiene una altura que me sorprendió, es famoso en la ciudad.

5 Ayer fuimos a limpiar un río, ... es muy profundo y está lleno de peces.

6 Tenemos que encontrar las salidas, ... están bastante lejos de aquí.

> **G**
> H The **relative pronouns** *el* ***cual***, *la* ***cual***, *los* ***cuales***, *las* ***cuales*** are another way to say 'who', 'which' or 'that'. They can refer to people of things and change in gender and number.
> *Esta es la razón por* ***la cual*** *estamos luchando.*

F **6 Translate these sentences into English.**

1 Soy una persona responsable. ....

2 Pienso mucho en los temas del medio ambiente. ....

3 Los cambios en el clima traen muchos riesgos. ....

4 Ayer escribí algunas opiniones en las redes sociales.

....

5 Tengo miedo de los fuegos que hay a veces en los bosques.

....

H **7 Translate this paragraph into Spanish on a separate sheet.**

I read articles about the culture of Latin America. I learned that many people protest to get justice. Everything possible should be done to help the people. I know that there are social problems that the government does not resolve. I hope that the people will not have many difficulties in the future.

Glossary

bold = this word will appear in Higher exams only

a pesar de	*despite, in spite of*
acceso (m)	*access*
acción (f)	*action*
actualmente	*currently, at present*
actuar	*(to) act, perform | acting, performing*
adoptar	*(to) adopt | adopting*
afectar	*(to) affect | affecting*
ahorrar	*(to) save (money, time, energy) | saving (money, time, energy)*
al aire libre	*outdoors*
algún	*a/an, any (m, before a noun)*
aliado (m), aliada (f)	*ally*
alimento (m)	*food, nourishment*
altura (f)	*height*
amarillo	*yellow*
ambiente (m)	*atmosphere*
anciano (m), anciana (f)	*old person*
andar	*(to) walk | walking*
anunciar	*(to) announce, advertise | announcing, advertising*
apagar	*(to) turn off, shut down | turning off, shutting down*
arreglar	*(to) repair, resolve | repairing, resolving*
artículo (m)	*article*
asociación (f)	*association*
ayuda (f)	*help*
ayudar	*(to) help | helping*
bajar	*(to) get off (mode of transport) go down, download, lower, reduce| getting off, going down, downloading, lowering, reducing*
bajo	*under, underneath*
bañar; bañarse	*to bathe | bathing; to have a bath, swim | bathing, swimming*
basarse (en)	*(to) be based (on) | being based (on)*
basta (+ infinitive)	*it's enough (to) + verb*
bicicleta (f)	*bicycle*
bolsa (f)	*(shopping) bag*
botella (f)	*bottle*
británico	*British*
caja (f)	*checkout, till, box*
cambio (m)	*change, exchange (money)*
campaña (f)	*campaign*
causa (f), **a causa de**	*cause, **because of***
causar	*(to) cause | causing*
cielo (m)	*sky*
ciudadano (m), ciudadana (f)	*citizen*
climático	*climate*
comentario (m)	*comment*
comercio (m)	*trade, business (shop)*
compañía (f)	*company, firm*
comportamiento (m)	*behaviour*
comunidad (f)	*community*

consecuencia (f)	*consequence*			
considerar	*(to) consider | considering*			
crisis (f)	*crisis*			
daño (m)	*damage, harm*			
de hecho	*actually, in fact*			
debate (m)	*debate*			
deber	*(to) have to, must | having to*			
debido a	*due to*			
defender	*(to) defend | defending*			
derecho (m)	*right*			
desaparecer	*(to) disappear | disappearing*			
destruir	*(to) destroy | destroying*			
di	*(I) gave*			
¡Di!	*Say!, Tell! (sing informal)*			
dieron	*(they) gave | (you (pl formal)) gave*			
dificultad (f)	*difficulty, obstacle*			
doy	*(I) give | (I) am giving*			
económico	*cheap, economic*			
educativo	*educational*			
efecto (m)	*effect*			
el cual, la cual, los cuales, las cuales	*that, which, who (m, f, mpl, fpl) (subj)*			
emergencia (f)	*emergency*			
esconder(se)	*(to) hide | hiding*			
esencial	*essential*			
esperar	*(to) hope, wait, expect | hoping, waiting, expecting*			
estabas	*(you (sing informal)) were | (you (sing informal)) used to be*			
explicación (f)	*explanation*			
expresión (f)	*expression*			
extraordinario	*extraordinary*			
famoso	*well-known, famous*			
figura (f)	*figure*			
final (m)	*end, ending, final*			
forma (f); en forma	*way, form, shape; fit, in shape*			
formar; formarse (en, como)	*(to) form | forming; (to) train (as) | training (as)*			
futuro (m)	*future*			
gobierno (m)	*government*			
grave	*serious, grave*			
¡Haz!	*Do!, Make! (sing informal)*			
humano	*human*			
igual	*equal, same as*			
influencia (f)	*influence*			
informar	*(to) inform | informing*			
intentar	*(to) try | trying*			
interés (m)	*interest*			
inundación (f)	*flood*			
isla (f)	*island*			
jefe (mf)	*boss, manager*			
justicia (f)	*justice, fairness*			
justo	*fair, just*			
juventud (f)	*youth*			
la	*her, it (f) (obj)*			
legal	*legal*			
libertad (f)	*freedom*			
limpiar	*(to) clean | cleaning*			
lluvia (f)	*rain*			
local	*local*			
lucha (f)	*fight*			
luchar	*(to) fight | fighting*			
manera (f)	*way*			
manifestación (f)	*protest*			
manifestarse	*(to) protest | protesting*			
material (m)	*material*			

medio ambiente (m)	*environment*
medios (mpl)	*media, means*
mencionar	*(to) mention | mentioning*
mercado (m)	*market*
merecer	*(to) deserve | deserving*
meter	*(to) put (into) | putting (into)*
(a) mí	*(to) me (emph)*
minoría (f)	*minority*
mostrar	*(to) show | showing*
mujer (f)	*woman, wife*
mundial	*global, world*
necesitar	*(to) need | needing*
nieve (f)	*snow*
no obstante	*however, nevertheless*
notar	*(to) notice | noticing*
nube (f)	*cloud*
nuestro	*our*
numeroso	*numerous*
objetivo (m)	*objective, goal*
objeto (m)	*object*
papel (m)	*paper, role, part (movie, play)*
parar(se); parar de (+ infinitive)	*(to) stop | stopping; (to) stop + verb (-ing) | stopping + verb (-ing)*
pasear	*(to) go for a walk, ride | going for a walk, riding*
pedir	*(to) ask for, order, request | asking for, ordering, requesting*
peligro (m)	*danger*
pena (f)	*shame, sadness*
periódico (m)	*newspaper*
personaje (m)	*character*
pez (m)	*fish*
plástico (m)	*plastic*
pobre	*poor*

poder (m)	*power*
polución (f)	*pollution*
¡Pon!; ¡Ponte!	*Put! (sing informal); Put on! (sing informal)*
poner; ponerse	*(to) put | putting; (to) put (on), get, become | putting (on), getting, becoming*
positivo	*positive*
premio (m)	*prize, reward*
presentación (f)	*presentation, introduction*
prestar	*(to) lend | lending*
principal	*main*
producir	*(to) produce | producing*
producto (m)	*product*
profundo	*deep, profound*
prohibir	*(to) forbid, ban | forbidding, banning*
proponer	*(to) propose, suggest | proposing, suggesting*
protección (f)	*protection*
proteger	*(to) protect | protecting*
proyecto (m)	*project, plan*
publicación (f)	*post, publication*
publicar	*(to) post (on the internet), publish | posting, publishing*
punto (m)	*point, full stop, dot*
quinto	*fifth*
racismo (m)	*racism*
reciclaje (m)	*recycling*
reciclar	*(to) recycle | recycling*
recoger	*(to) pick up, tidy up | picking up, tidying up*
recursos (mpl)	*resources*
renovable	*renewable*

Spanish	English
resultado (m)	*result, outcome*
rojo	*red*
¡Sal!	*Leave! (sing informal)*
salida (f)	*exit, departure*
saltar; saltarse	*(to) jump | jumping; (to) break (rule), skip (class), jump (queue) | breaking (rule), skipping (class), jumping (queue)*
¡Sé...!	*Be...! (sing informal)*
seco	*dry*
ser (m)	*being*
servicio (m)	*service, toilet*
sexismo (m)	*sexism*
sino	*but, rather*
situación (f)	*situation*
sociedad (f)	*society*
solo	*alone*
solución (f)	*solution*
sorpresa (f)	*surprise*
suerte (f)	*luck*
supermercado (m)	*supermarket*
temporada (f)	*season (period of time, TV, series, food...)*
¡Ten...!	*Have! (sing informal)*
tenga; tenga que	*(I) have (subjunctive) | (she, he, it, one) has (subjunctive) | you (sing formal)) have (subjunctive); have to, must (subjunctive) | has to, must (subjunctive) | have to, must (subjunctive)*
tengas; tengas que	*(you (sing informal)) have (subjunctive); have to, must (subjunctive)*
tierra (f)	*earth, land, ground*
universal	*universal*
vale la pena (+ infinitive)	*it's worth it (to)*
vaya; me vaya (de), se vaya (de)	*(I) go (subjunctive) | (she, he, it, one) goes (subjunctive) | (you (sing formal)) go (subjunctive); leave (subjunctive) | leaves (subjunctive) | leave (subjunctive)*
¡Ve!; **¡Vete (de)!**	*Go! (sing informal);* ***Leave! (sing informal)***
vehículo (m)	*vehicle*
¡Ven!	*Come! (sing informal)*
vender	*(to) sell | selling*
verdadero	*real, true*
versión (f)	*version*
víctima (mf)	*victim, casualty*
vidrio (m)	*glass, pane*
votar	*(to) vote | voting*
voz (f)	*voice*

Zona de cultura Pioneros latinos

Using different tenses to talk about the past

1 These sentences are written in the past. Decide whether they are written in the imperfect (I), preterite (Pr) or perfect tense (P).

1 El artista vivía en Madrid en 2010. ....
2 Mi amiga conoció a su novio el año pasado. ....
3 He ganado mucho dinero este año. ....
4 El policía tuvo que ir al extranjero ayer. ....
5 Había muchos clientes en la empresa. ....
6 Ya he preparado todo para ir al trabajo. ....

> **G** When talking about the past, use the **imperfect tense** to describe something or say what someone used to do, the **preterite tense** to say what someone did and the **perfect tense** to say what someone has done.

2 Underline the verbs in the past tenses in the passage. There are four verbs in each tense: preterite, imperfect and perfect. Write each verb in the correct group below.

El año pasado decidí ir a otro país para tener una nueva experiencia. Compré un billete de ida y vuelta y cogí el avión a Ecuador. Allí había un colegio que quería profesores de países diferentes. Cada día trabajaba y ayudaba a los niños. Al final tuve que volver para continuar mis estudios, pero sé que he aprendido mucho. Ahora he decidido que no quiero ser actriz. He escogido estudiar ciencias y ahora, porque he visto una parte diferente del mundo, tengo ganas de trabajar para intentar mejorar el medio ambiente.

Preterite: 1 .... 2 .... 3 .... 4 ....
Imperfect: 1 .... 2 .... 3 .... 4 ....
Perfect: 1 .... 2 .... 3 .... 4 ....

3 Circle the most appropriate verb tense to complete each sentence.

1 Yo nunca **he estado** / **estaba** en las Islas Canarias.
2 Mi tío no **reconocía** / **reconoció** a su prima después de muchos años.
3 Pilar todavía no **respondía** / **ha respondido** a mi mensaje.
4 Antes mi abuela **tenía** / **ha tenido** una buena carrera.
5 La doctora me **dio** / **daba** unas medicinas hace dos semanas.
6 Cuando era más joven, yo no **quería** / **he querido** ir a la universidad.
H 7 Me **he acordado** / Me **acordaba** del examen que tengo mañana.
H 8 Ahora soy capaz de correr muchos kilómetros, pero no **estuve** / **estaba** en forma cuando era más joven.

4 Complete the sentences with an appropriate tense of the verb in brackets.

1 El año pasado el escritor latino .... mucho éxito. (*tener*)
2 Cuando eras pequeño, ¿que .... en verano? (*hacer*)
3 El actor .... en un supermercado cuando comenzó su carrera. (*trabajar*)
4 Esa señora ya .... mucho dinero como modelo. (*ganar*)
5 Yo .... al colegio cuando vi al director. (*llegar*)

H 6 En las últimas semanas .... con varios compañeros de clase sobre la salud mental. (*conversar*)

H 7 Antes de buscar un empleo, Diego .... pasar tiempo en un país en Latinoamérica. (*querer*)

H 5 Rewrite each sentence, putting the words into the correct order.

1 al después ayuda Agradecí de su ayer la por médico cita

....

2 familia Siempre una he tener deseado

....

3 siempre Antes con efectivo pagaba

....

4 negó El a sus niño se deberes hacer

....

5 dinero Mi negocio padre ha mucho en gastado ese

....

6 ¿eras Tú mucho cuando te joven preocupabas?

....

F 6 Translate these sentences into Spanish.

1 I like that Colombian actor.

....

2 I watch his films every weekend.

....

3 Last year I started following him on social media.

....

4 He has had a lot of success in the world of cinema.

....

5 I think it is important to relax in your free time.

....

H 7 Translate this paragraph into English.

El artista viene de un barrio pobre. Comprendo su mensaje cuando escucho su música. Empezó su carrera cantando en la calle para ganar dinero. Hoy en día todavía apoya a su madre enferma y a su familia. Me encanta su música porque trata de las condiciones sociales que él entiende bien.

....

....

....

....

1 Sueños y esperanzas

- Using different ways to express future plans
- **H** Using *cuando* + present subjunctive

1 Complete each sentence using a word from the box.

1 Me gustaría .... una familia en el futuro.

2 Espero trabajar duro y .... un buen salario.

3 Voy a .... a la universidad.

4 Quiero .... muchas lenguas.

5 También espero .... a salvar el planeta.

6 Me gustaría .... por el mundo.

G To talk about **future plans**, you can use the following expressions followed by the infinitive:
me gustaría, espero, quiero, voy a, tengo ganas de, **H** *tengo la intención de.*

ayudar	viajar	ganar
hablar	tener	ir

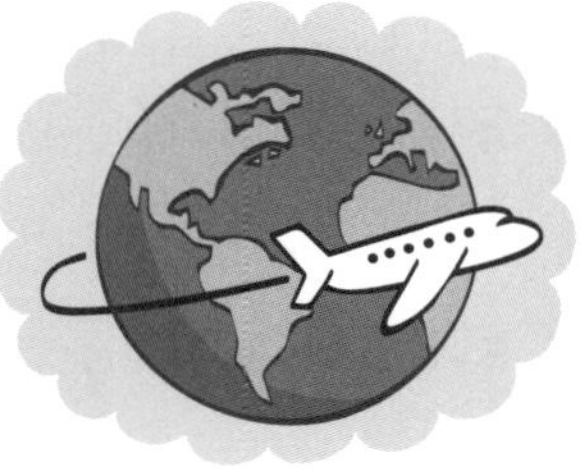

2 Complete the sentences with the 'I' form of the simple future tense of the verb in brackets.

1 En dos años .... un coche eléctrico. (*comprar*)

2 .... a España para mejorar mi castellano. (*ir*)

3 Creo que .... más tiempo libre. (*tener*)

4 .... unas decisiones grandes sobre mi carrera. (*tomar*)

5 El año próximo .... hacer más ejercicio. (*poder*)

6 Después de mis estudios, ... un trabajo interesante. (*buscar*)

G You can also use the **simple future tense**. It is formed using the infinitive with the future endings (**-é**, **-ás**, **-á**), but remember that there are some irregular stems: *tendré, haré, podré, pondré,* and *habrá* (there will be).

3 Complete these sentences by translating the words in brackets.

1 .... (*I want to*) visitar muchos otros países del mundo.

2 .... (*I am going to*) trabajar en una oficina.

3 .... (*I hope to*) casarme con alguien simpático.

4 .... (*I would like to*) integrarme en un buen equipo de trabajo.

5 .... (*I am keen on*) compartir un piso con amigos.

H 6 .... (*I intend to*) ganar un buen salario.

H 7 .... (*I will pursue*) todos mis sueños.

G Use 'if' clauses to talk about future plans that depend on something else.
Si + **present**, + **future time phrase**
Si ***voy*** *a la universidad,* ***encontraré*** *un buen trabajo.*

4 Draw lines to match up the sentence halves.

1 Si mi hermana tiene éxito en sus exámenes,
2 Si tenemos una casa más grande,
3 Si llego a encontrar un trabajo,
4 Si tengo un buen plan,
5 Si viajo a España, necesitaré
H 6 Si tengo suficientes seguidores,
H 7 Si consigo aprender español,
H 8 Si puedo pertenecer al club,

a tendré mi propia habitación.
b veré claro mi futuro.
c seguiré jugando en el equipo.
d seré famoso y me marcharé a la gran ciudad.
e espero lograr mi sueño de vivir en España.
f voy a trabajar muy duro.
g quiere ir a la universidad.
h cambiar mi dinero de pesos a euros.

G

H When talking about future plans after the word *cuando*, remember to use the **present subjunctive** instead of the present simple:
*Cuando **tenga** niños ...* *Cuando **vaya** al extranjero ...*

H 5 Complete the sentences with the correct subjunctive form of the verb in brackets.

1 Cuando .... mayor, a mí me gustaría experimentar otras culturas. (*ser*)
2 Cuando tú .... a mi casa, podremos ver la nueva película. (*venir*)
3 Voy a comprarme un coche cuando .... más dinero. (*tener*)
4 Cuando mi hermana .... su examen, seguro que va a equivocarse. (*hacer*)
5 Espero poder comunicarme con la gente cuando .... al extranjero. (*ir*)

F 6 Translate these sentences into English.

1 Quiero ir a la universidad. ....
2 Después de estudiar, espero encontrar un trabajo.
....
3 Si tengo suerte, puedo ganar dinero y viajar. ....
4 Recientemente visité a mi tía que vive en otro continente.
....
5 Ella comprende el castellano y siempre lo pasamos muy bien.
....

H 7 Translate this paragraph into Spanish.

I am keen to have children when I am older. If I have time, I want to travel before I get married. My brother is an entrepreneur with his own business. I have done training in a local industry. My boss has lots of experience and I will continue working there this year.

....
....
....
....

2 ¡A trabajar!

Using *para/sin* + infinitive • H Using possessive pronouns

1 Circle the correct verb to complete each sentence.

1 **Hago** / **Trabajo** en una tienda.

2 **Odio** / **Me gusta** mi trabajo porque es bastante divertido.

3 **Gano** / **Tengo** diez euros por hora.

4 **Me llevo** / **Discuto** bien con mi jefa porque es agradable.

5 **Necesito** / **Hago** el trabajo los sábados.

6 Me gustaría **haber** / **tener** un trabajo con más responsabilidad en el futuro.

2 Draw lines to match up each problem with the appropriate advice.

1 Me duele la cabeza.

2 No tengo dinero.

3 Me siento solo porque soy hijo único.

4 Nunca tengo éxito en el colegio.

5 Paso demasiado tiempo en las redes.

6 No duermo bien.

a Hay que pedir ayuda al profesor.

b No hay que mirar el móvil por la noche.

c Tienes que buscar un trabajo.

d Tienes que ir al doctor.

e Tienes que adoptar un gato o un perro.

f Hay que salir y hacer más ejercicio.

G

The prepositions ***para*** and ***sin*** are often followed by an infinitive.
para + infinitive = in order to (do) ***sin*** + infinitive = without (doing)
para *estudiar* **in order to** study ***sin*** *poder dormir* **without** being able to sleep
H ***Antes de*** and ***después de*** work in the same way.
antes de + infinitive = before (doing) ***después de*** + infinitive = after (doing)
antes de *salir* **before** going out ***después de*** *comer* **after** eating

3 Read Marta's blog about her part-time job. Complete the text using words from the box.

Tengo que .... que odio mi trabajo. Lo hago para .... dinero porque quiero .... una bicicleta. Trabajo ocho horas sin .... y por eso lo quiero .... Mi jefa no es simpática y a veces tengo que .... los servicios. La verdad es que es terrible.

H Sin embargo, mi pasión es el deporte y quiero .... empleo en el centro deportivo. Después de .... este trabajo, ¡no me apetece nunca más trabajar en un restaurante!

tener
comprar
limpiar
decir
ganar
dejar
solicitar
descansar

4 Rewrite these sentences, translating the English phrases into Spanish.

1 Voy al Reino Unido *in order to visit* a mi abuela. ....

2 Mi hermano no podía hablar *without laughing*. ....

3 El hombre corre muchos riesgos *without thinking* en el futuro. ....

4 Quiero comparar los precios *in order not to pay* demasiado. ....

H 5 *Before checking* la cuenta en el bar, el hombre habló con el jefe. ....

H 6 *After assisting* al último cliente, la señora se fue a casa. ....

G

H Possessive pronouns are used to avoid repetition.

singular		plural	
el mío / la mía el tuyo / la tuya el suyo / la suya	el nuestro / la nuestra el vuestro / la vuestra el suyo / la suya	los míos / las mías los tuyos / las tuyas los suyos / las suyas	los nuestros/ las nuestras los vuestros / las vuestras los suyos / las suyas

H 5 Complete these sentences with the correct form of the possessive pronoun in brackets.

1 Tus diseños son artísticos, pero .... son decepcionantes. (*mine*)

2 No me gusta ese presidente, prefiero .... (*ours*)

3 Estas novelas no me interesan nada, creo que .... son muy buenas. (*his*)

4 Mi empresa tiene problemas, pero .... ha tenido éxito este año. (*yours* (*inf*) *sing*)

5 ¿Has visto su colección? .... es mejor. (*yours* (*inf*) *plural*)

6 Creo que los científicos aquí saben mucho, pero .... saben aún más. (*theirs*)

F 6 Translate these sentences into Spanish.

1 I work in a shop on Sundays.

....

2 I get on well with my boss.

....

3 The work is boring and the hours are long.

....

4 Last week, I bought a new dress.

....

5 I want to earn money to go on holiday.

....

H 7 Translate this paragraph into English.

Tengo un trabajo en una empresa en la ciudad. Antes de comenzar aquí, trabajaba en otra oficina. Quiero solicitar un nuevo trabajo porque tengo dudas sobre lo que hago. En realidad, pienso que mi jefa quiere sustituirme, lo que me da miedo. Por lo tanto, voy a buscar una nueva oportunidad en otra industria.

....

....

....

....

3 Un trabajo para todos

Using masculine and feminine nouns for jobs

1 Read what the young people say about themselves and write the most appropriate profession from the box. There are more professions than gaps.

1 Carla: Quiero ayudar a personas enfermas. Quiero ser ....

2 Marco: Me encanta pintar. Quiero ser ....

3 Amira: Desde niña siempre he cantando. Quiero ser ....

4 Emilio: Quiero trabajar en una escuela. Quiero ser ....

5 Sara: Me encantan las palabras. Quiero ser ....

artista
escritor
cantante
profesor
doctora
escritora
profesora
doctor

2 Draw lines to match up the sentence halves.

1 Me gusta la idea

2 No tengo ganas de

3 Mi sueño es hacer

4 Quiero ser

5 Me gustaría ir

a un trabajo al aire libre.

b a otro país.

c trabajar con los animales.

d de ser policía.

e profesora de universidad.

G

Some nouns have different masculine and feminine forms.
medico → *médic**a***
*escrit**or*** → *escrit**ora***
Nouns ending in ***-e*** or ***-ista*** are usually **invariable**: *agent**e***, *art**ista***.

3 Rewrite the sentences, changing the gender of the nouns in bold. Remember to check articles and adjectives that need to agree with the noun.

1 Mi sueño es ser **profesor** y trabajar con los niños.

....

2 Me gusta la idea de trabajar desde casa y ser independiente como, por ejemplo, **una escritora**.

....

3 Quiero hacer un trabajo con responsabilidad, como **una policía**.

....

4 Me interesa ser **actor** porque quiero ser famoso.

....

5 Prefiero ser **directora** de empresa y tener un buen salario.

....

H 6 A ella le gustaría tener una reunión con **la presidenta** de su empresa.

....

H 7 Me apetece trabajar con mis **compañeros** en el extranjero.

....

4 Complete the sentences with a noun that corresponds to the adjective given in brackets.

Example: La ..seguridad.. en las calles es importante. (*seguro*)

> The suffix ***-dad*** or ***-idad*** is often added to an adject ve in Spanish to form a noun (the word in English would usually end in '-ty' or '-ity'). These words are always feminine.

1 La directora toma muy en serio su .... (*responsable*)

2 Es importante luchar por la .... de género. (*igual*)

3 En ...., no todo el mundo está en contra del uso del *streaming*. (*real*)

H 4 Existe la .... de una temperatura mínima de treinta grados mañana. (*posible*)

H 5 Durante la fiesta, había mucha .... (*feliz*)

H **5 Complete the diary entry with the words from the box. There are more words than gaps.**

Estoy buscando un nuevo empleo. Tengo que asegurarme de encontrar el trabajo perfecto. Tengo la .... de llevarme bien con mis compañeros de trabajo, los .... en mi trabajo actual son simpáticos y .... apoyo mucho. Quiero un trabajo con más ...., dado que tengo muchos conocimientos. Trabajar en una nueva empresa me dará mucha .... en mi vida laboral.

felicidad
capacidad
responsabilidad
identidad
cuales
nacionalidad
igualdad
las los
posibilidad
suyos
míos
calidades

F **6 Translate these sentences into English.**

1 Tengo un trabajo en un parque. ....

2 Me importa la responsabilidad que tengo. ....

3 Antes trabajaba en una empresa muy grande. ....

4 Es una buena experiencia pasar el día al aire libre.

....

5 Quiero seguir mis sueños en el futuro. ....

H **7 Translate this paragraph into Spanish.**

I am keen on becoming a doctor. I have chosen to care for sick people I want to work in a hospital, but I don't mind about the salary. My brother has been studying for a couple of years on his course. I know that mine is going to be much longer than his.

....

....

....

....

4 Las lenguas te abren las puertas

Using modal verbs • Using different verb forms

1 Draw lines to match up the sentences with the times using the 24-hour clock.

1 El tren llega a las catorce cincuenta.	**a** 12.25
2 El autobús sale a las veinte cuarenta y cinco.	**b** 14.50
3 El avión llega a las doce veinticinco.	**c** 19.30
4 El tren sale a las veintidós quince.	**d** 22.15
5 El avión llega a las diecinueve treinta.	**e** 10.04
6 El autobús llega a las diez cero cuatro.	**f** 20.45

2 Rewrite these sentences, translating the English words into Spanish.

> **G** An **<u>infinitive</u>** can be used as a noun where English uses a word ending in '-ing'.
> ***<u>estudiar</u>*** *es importante* — **studying** is important
> ***<u>fumar</u>*** *está prohibido* — **smoking** is forbidden

1 *Speaking* otras lenguas es divertido.

....

2 Es útil *learning* una nueva lengua. ....

3 *Understanding* otras culturas es importante. ....

4 *Carrying on* con tus estudios puede ser difícil. ....

5 *Travelling* a otro país es más fácil si hablas la lengua. ....

6 *Improving* mi castellano es una buena idea. ....

> **G** **Modal verbs** are followed by the <u>infinitive</u>. They include:

deber (debo)	to have to	*poder (puedo)*	to be able to
querer (quiero)	to want to	*saber (sé)*	to know (how to)
tener que (tengo que)	to have to		

3 Complete each sentence using the correct form of the modal verb in brackets. Pay attention to the tenses.

1 Ellos .... aprender una nueva lengua. (*deber*)

2 ¿Tú .... escribir más detalles? (*poder*)

3 Yo .... ir a mi restaurante habitual ayer. (*querer*)

4 El padre .... dar más independencia a su hijo. (*tener que*)

5 Nosotros .... pronunciar las palabras en castellano. (*saber*)

6 Ellas .... escoger un nuevo tema. (*querer*)

H 7 Mi madre .... mandar un saludo a su hermana mañana. (*querer*)

H 8 Yo .... regalarle algo a mi abuela porque es su cumpleaños. (*deber*)

4 Complete the blog post using the correct form of the verbs from the box. You will need to decide on the correct tense and person for each gap.

Ahora estoy .... una nueva lengua. La razón es que ya sé .... castellano e inglés, y quiero comprender más lenguas para poder ir a trabajar al extranjero. Cuando .... a Barcelona, ... con mucha gente y fue emocionante. Tengo que .... mucho tiempo estudiando para .... mi nivel. A mi edad, es importante pensar en el futuro.

H Me atrevo a decir que .... éxito, dado que la enseñanza en mi colegio es absolutamente increíble. Mi profesora se .... con el trabajo que le he dado y tiene una buena impresión de mí.

mejorar
aprender
pasar
hablar
tener
ir
sorprender

G

Verbs ending in ***-ger*** or ***-cer*** / ***-cir*** have an irregular 'I' form in the present tense:

*co**ger*** →	*co**jo***	(I take)	**H** *agrade**cer*** →	*agrade**zco***	(I thank)
*esco**ger*** →	*esco**jo***	(I choose)	**H** *tradu**cir*** →	*tradu**zco***	(I translate)
*cono**cer*** →	*cono**zco***	(I know)	**H** *produ**cir*** →	*produ**zco***	(I produce)

H 5 Complete the sentences with the 'I' form of the verb in brackets.

1 .... a tu prima. Es muy simpática y hermosa. (*conocer*)

2 Después de comprar un billete, ... el primer tren que sale. (*coger*)

3 .... el pago a mi cuenta cuando el precio es más bajo. (*reducir*)

4 .... a mis amigos universitarios por su apoyo. (*agradecer*)

5 .... novelas del inglés al español. (*traducir*)

6 .... el tamaño más grande. (*elegir*)

7 Siempre .... resultados positivos en mi empresa. (*producir*)

F 6 Translate these sentences into Spanish.

1 Learning languages is fun and important. ....

2 I know how to speak Spanish and English. ....

3 I want to travel abroad in the future. ....

4 I know someone who has been to the Canary Islands.

....

5 Last week I studied a new topic at school. ....

H 7 Translate this paragraph into English.

Llevo seis meses viviendo aquí. Tengo que usar otro idioma en mi vida diaria y en el colegio. Desde el principio, elegí hablar castellano con mis amigos. Mi madre está orgullosa porque es consciente de las dificultades que tengo. A veces me equivoco, pero sé que estoy haciendo avances y soy feliz.

....

....

....

....

5 El trabajo antes, ahora … y mañana

Using different tenses to talk about changes in the world of work

1 Read the sentences about Spain and write out the percentages in numbers.

1 A finales de los años 1890, el sesenta y seis por ciento de la gente trabajaba en el campo. ....

2 A finales de los años sesenta, el cincuenta y tres por ciento trabajaba en el turismo. ....

3 En 2023, solo el cuatro por ciento trabajaba en la tierra. ....

4 Hoy en día, el setenta y cinco por ciento de la gente trabaja en servicios. ....

5 Ahora el sesenta y cuatro por ciento de los españoles sabe usar el ordenador. ....

2 Complete the sentences using the correct future form (*ir a* + infinitive) of the verb in brackets.

1 ¿Te .... los calcetines, por favor, Marcos? (*put on*)

2 Yo .... un billete de ida en la estación esta tarde. (*buy*)

3 (Nosotros) .... muchos dólares con nosotros. (*take*)

4 La profesora .... la mitad de las monedas a una buena causa. (*give*)

5 Los señores .... al aeropuerto a las ocho. (*go in*)

6 ¿Vosotras .... un tren directo desde Madrid para el viaje de vuelta? (*catch*)

3 Draw lines to match up each question with the correct answer.

1 ¿Dónde trabajaste el año pasado?

2 ¿Qué tipo de trabajo quieres hacer?

3 ¿Dónde vas a trabajar en el futuro?

4 ¿Has tenido un trabajo ya?

5 ¿Cómo era el mundo profesional en el pasado?

H 6 ¿Enseñarás a niños en el futuro?

H 7 ¿Tu empleo actual es en una agencia?

a Voy a ser profesora en un colegio.

b Era más fácil encontrar trabajo.

c No, trabajo en un hospital.

d Quiero hacer un trabajo al aire libre.

e Sí, he trabajado en un restaurante.

f No, tendré un empleo trabajando con animales.

g Trabajé en una oficina.

> **G** The **imperfect tense** describes what someone was doing or used to do in the past. In the singular, **-*ar*** verbs end in **-*aba***, **-*abas***, **-*aba***; **-*er*** and **-*ir*** verbs end in **-*ía***, **-*ías***, **-*ía***. Only three verbs are irregular in the imperfect – ***ser*** (*era*), ***ir*** (*iba*) and ***ver*** (*veía*).

4 Complete the sentences using the imperfect tense of the verb in brackets.

1 En el pasado, ... más trabajo en los campos. (*haber*)

2 La gente no .... tantas opciones como hoy. (*tener*)

3 Yo .... muy claro los problemas del mundo del trabajo. (*ver*)

4 Mi padre .... a su empresa todos los días. (*ir*)

5 Tú no .... trabajar desde casa. (*poder*)

H 6 En el mundo laboral, no .... muchas leyes civiles para proteger a la gente. (*existir*)

H 7 Los jefes siempre nos .... un plazo corto para hacer encuestas importantes. (*dar*)

H 5 Circle the correct form of the simple future tense to complete each sentence.

1 Creo que la compañía **alcanzará / llegará** un nivel más alto este año.

2 Mi jefa **hará / buscará** una búsqueda en línea para tener la información.

3 Nosotros **perseguiremos / proporcionaremos** más productos al público el año próximo.

4 El desarrollo de la empresa **tendrá / será** una señal de su éxito.

5 Un aspecto positivo de trabajar aquí es que mi jefa me aprecia y eso no **cambiará / durará**.

6 Sea lo que sea, **seré / seguiré** trabajando aquí debido a la falta de empleos en mi barrio.

7 Un título universitario **aprovechará / traerá** más seguridad en el trabajo.

F 6 Translate these sentences into English.

1 Tengo un trabajo en el campo.

2 Todos los días salgo de casa a las siete.

3 Estoy contento de pasar el día al aire libre.

4 Hace dos años trabajaba en una tienda.

5 El sesenta por ciento de la gente vive en las ciudades.

H 7 Translate this paragraph into Spanish.

I have lived near the border for a decade. Unfortunately, there is a lack of work in the region. My sister fell in love with a local girl last year. Soon they are going to celebrate their union with a party. We have many happy occasions with the family here.

6 El futuro sin límites

- Using the simple future tense in the 'he/she/it' form
- H Using *para que* + present subjunctive

1 Circle the correct form of the future tense to complete each sentence.

1 En el futuro el ordenador **podrá** / **será** más importante.

2 Yo **tendré** / **tendrá** un buen trabajo.

3 Creo que **pondré** / **habrá** más transporte eléctrico.

4 Yo **hablarás** / **hablaré** con gente en otros países por Internet cada día.

5 **Podré** / **Pondré** usar la tecnología del futuro en mi trabajo.

G

To use the **simple future tense**, add the endings **-é**, **-ás**, **-á** to the infinitive. Remember that some verbs have an irregular stem: *tener* (***tendr**é*), *hacer* (***har**é*), *poder* (***podr**é*), *poner* (***pondr**é*), and *habr**á*** = 'there will be'.

2 Rewrite each sentence, putting the words into the correct order.

1 en de trabajar porque Estoy línea favor es a útil

....

2 muchas En habrá futuro cámaras el

....

3 ayudará Creo Internet a que estudiantes los

....

4 usar No tiempo debe se móvil todo el el

....

5 la Estoy uso de tecnología en personas vez de contra del en

....

3 Complete the sentences using the correct article. Write X if no article is needed.

1 Fui al cine con .... amigos ayer.

2 Mi padre es .... doctor, pero a él no le gusta .... gente enferma.

3 ¿Tu casa no tiene .... jardín?

H 4 Voy a hacer .... visitas breves a mis familiares.

H 5 Mi primo tiene .... características muy positivas.

H 6 Hay .... concepto que no entiendo bien.

4 Write down the infinitive of the conjugated verb(s) used in each sentence.

1 Estoy durmiendo en casa. ....

2 Mi hermano hará sus deberes más tarde. ....

3 Me visto la ropa por la mañana. ....

4 ¿Tendrás tiempo para salir esta noche? ....

H 5 Me han cobrado veinte euros – ¡me han robado! ....

H 6 La científica está inventando algo nuevo. ....

H 7 La situación reflejará lo que hizo el director anterior. ....

G

H You use the **present subjunctive** after ***para que*** ('so that', 'in order that') to express purpose where the subject of the verb changes.
Ayudamos a los niños ***para que tengan*** *una buena educación.*
We help the children **so that** they **have** a good education.
Where the subject of the verb is the same in both parts of the sentence, simply use ***para*** + infinitive.
Ayudamos a los niños ***para*** *cambiar el mundo.*
We help the children **in order to** change the world.

H 5 Complete these sentences with the correct form of the present subjunctive. Then translate each sentence into English.

1 Voy a llamar al agente para que él .... el trabajo. (*hacer*)

....

2 La empresa está aumentando mi salario anual para que yo .... jefe de oficina. (*ser*)

....

3 Cuando .... a mi casa, conocerás a mis dos hermanas: ambas son muy simpáticas. (*venir*)

....

4 A ti te falta estudiar para que .... buenos resultados. (*tener*)

....

5 A ellos les importa la buena educación para que su hijo .... a la universidad. (*ir*)

F 6 Translate these sentences into Spanish.

1 I do my homework online. ....

2 I like spending time on my mobile phone. ....

3 My cousin works a lot with computers. ....

4 I went to visit a university with my parents. ....

5 I want to study technology because it is changing the world

....

H 7 Translate this paragraph into English.

El futuro tiene posibilidades para todos. Mis hermanas quieren casarse; a ellas les importa tener hijos. Yo tengo la idea contraria porque prefiero volar alrededor del mundo. Mi amigo habla mucho de su viaje del año pasado, que a él le encantó. En mi opinión, es fundamental siempre seguir tus sueños para ser feliz.

....

....

....

....

Glossary

bold = this word will appear in Higher exams only

absolutamente	*absolutely*
acordarse (de)	*(to) remember | remembering*
actor (m)	*actor (m)*
actriz (f)	*actress, actor (f)*
actual	*current*
agencia (f)	*agency*
agente (mf)	*agent, officer*
agradecer	*(to) thank | thanking*
al / en el extranjero	*abroad*
alcanzar	*(to) reach | reaching*
ambos	*both*
anterior	*previous, preceding*
antes; **antes de (+ infinitive)**	*before;* ***beforehand | before (+ -ing)***
anual	*yearly, annual*
artista (mf)	*artist*
apoyar	*(to) support | supporting*
asegurarse de	*(to) ensure | ensuring*
aspecto (m)	*aspect, appearance*
atender	*(to) assist (customer), serve | assisting (customer), serving*
atreverse	*(to) dare | daring*
avance (m)	*advance, progress*
bar (m)	*bar*
billete (m)	*ticket (transport), note (money)*
billete de ida (m)	*single ticket*
billete de ida y vuelta (m)	*return ticket*
breve	*brief, short*
búsqueda (f)	*search*
calcetín (m)	*sock*
capacidad (f)	*ability, capacity*
capaz	*capable, able*
característica (f)	*characteristic, quality*
carrera (f)	*career, university degree, race*
castellano (m)	*(Castilian) Spanish*
científico (m), científica (f)	*scientist*
civil	*civil*
cliente (mf)	*customer*
cobrar	*(to) charge (money) | charging (money)*
colección (f)	*collection*
compañero (m), compañera (f)	*classmate, companion, colleague*
comparar	*(to) compare | comparing*
comprender	*(to) understand | understanding*
comprobar	*(to) check | checking*
comunicar, comunicarse	*(to) communicate | communicating*
concepto (m)	*concept*
condición (f)	*condition*
conocer	*(to) know, meet, experience | knowing, meeting, experiencing*
conocimiento (m)	*knowledge*
consciente	*conscious, aware*
continente (m)	*continent*
continuar; **continuar + present participle**	*(to) continue, carry on | continuing, carrying on;* ***(to) continue to, still be + -ing | continuing to***

contrario	*contrary, opposite*
conversar	*(to) chat, talk | chatting, talking*
dado (que)	*given (that)*
década (f)	*decade*
decisión (f)	*decision*
demasiado	*too much*
desarrollo (m)	*development, progress*
desear	*(to) wish | wishing*
detalle (m)	*detail*
dinero (m)	*money*
directo	*direct, straight*
director (m), directora (f)	*boss, headteacher*
diseño (m)	*design*
doctor (m), doctora (f)	*doctor*
dólar (m)	*dollar*
duda (f)	*doubt*
edad (f)	*age*
efectivo (m)	*cash*
eléctrico	*electric*
elegir	*(to) choose | choosing*
él | **(a) él**	*he (subj) |* ***(to) him, it (m) (emph)***
ella | **(a) ella**	*she (subj) |* ***(to) her, it (f) (emph)***
ellas | **(a) ellas**	*they (f) (subj) |* ***(to) them (f) (emph)***
ellos | **(a) ellos**	*they (m, mixed gender) (subj) |* ***(to) them (m, mixed gender) (emph)***
empleo (m)	*job, employment*
empresa (f)	*company (firm)*
empresario (m), empresaria (f)	*entrepreneur, manager, employer*
enamorar(se)	*(to) fall in love | falling in love*
encuesta (f)	*survey*
enseñanza (f)	*teaching*
enseñar	*(to) teach, show | teaching, showing*
entrar	*(to) enter, go in | entering, going in*
equivocarse	*(to) be wrong, make a mistake | being wrong, making a mistake*
escoger	*(to) choose | choosing*
escritor (m), escritora (f)	*writer*
existir	*(to) exist | existing*
éxito (m)	*success*
experiencia (f)	*experience*
experimentar	*(to) experience | experiencing*
falta (+ infinitive)	*it's/is still to be (+ pp)*
falta (de) (f)	*lack (of), shortage*
favor (m); por favor	*favour; please*
felicidad (f)	*happiness*
frontera (f)	*border, frontier*
fundamental	*essential*
ganar	*(to) win, earn | winning, earning*
grado (m)	*degree*
habitual	*usual*
habrá	*there will be | there is going to be*
idioma (m)	*language (specific language)*
impresión (f)	*impression*
independencia (f)	*independence*
industria (f)	*industry, factory*
integrar, integrarse	*(to) integrate | integrating*
intención (f)	*intention*
inventar	*(to) invent | inventing*
jefa (f)	*boss, manager*

laboral	*work, working, labour*
latino	*Latin*
lengua (f)	*tongue, language*
ley (f)	*law*
llegar; llegar a + inf.	*(to) arrive / arriving; (to) manage to / managing to*
lograr	*(to) achieve, succeed, manage / achieving, succeeding, managing*
Madrid (m)	*Madrid*
marcharse	*(to) leave, go away / leaving, going away*
me apetece + inf. /noun	*I feel like + -ing / noun*
me da igual	*I don't mind, I'm not bothered*
médico (m), médica (f)	*doctor*
mínimo	*minimum*
mío, mía, míos, mías	*mine (m, f, mpl, fpl)*
el mío, la mía, los míos, las mías	*mine (m, f, mpl, fpl)*
mitad (f)	*half*
modelo (mf)	*model*
moneda (f)	*coin, currency*
mundo (m)	*world*
negarse a	*(to) refuse / refusing*
negocio (m)	*business, store*
el nuestro, la nuestra, los nuestros, las nuestras	*ours*
ocasión (f)	*occasion*
ocuparse (de)	*(to) look after, take care of / looking after, taking care of*
oficina (f)	*office*
oportunidad (f)	*opportunity, chance*
pago (m)	*payment*
país (m)	*country*
palabra (f)	*word*
par (m)	*pair, couple*
para que	*so that, in order to*
para; para (+ infinitive)	*for; in order to (+ verb)*
perseguir	*(to) pursue / pursuing*
pertenecer	*(to) belong / belonging*
peso (m)	*peso (currency)*
plan (m)	*plan*
planeta (m)	*planet*
plazo (m)	*deadline, instalment*
policía (mf)	*police, police force, police officer*
por lo tanto	*therefore*
preocupar(se) (de, por)	*(to) worry / worrying*
preparar, prepararse	*(to) prepare / preparing; (to) prepare oneself, get ready / preparing oneself, getting ready*
presidenta (f)	*president, chairperson*
presidente (m)	*president, chairperson*
principio (m)	*start, beginning*
pronunciar	*(to) pronounce / pronouncing*
propio	*own*
proporcionar	*(to) provide, supply / providing, supplying*
razón (f)	*reason, right, correct*
realidad (f)	*reality*
reconocer	*(to) recognise, admit / recognising, admitting*
reflejar	*(to) reflect / reflecting*

		😕	🙂	😎
regalar	*(to) give (as a present) | giving (as a present)*			
Reino Unido (m)	*United Kingdom*			
reír(se)	*(to) laugh | laughing*			
responder	*(to) answer | answering*			
responsabilidad (f)	*responsibility*			
reunión (f)	*meeting, reunion*			
riesgo (m)	*risk*			
robar	*(to) steal, rob | stealing, robbing*			
salario (m)	*salary, wage*			
saludo (m)	*greeting, regards*			
salvar	*(to) save, rescue | saving, rescuing*			
sea	*(I) am (subjunctive) | (she, he, it one) is (subjunctive) | (you (sing formal)) are (subjunctive)*			
seguir; **seguir + present participle**	*(to) follow, continue | following, continuing;* ***(to) continue to, still be + -ing | continuing to***			
seguridad (f)	*security, safety*			
señal (f)	*sign (road sign)*			
simpático	*nice, kind, friendly*			
sin embargo	*however, nevertheless*			
sin, sin (+ infinitive)	*without, without (+ -ing)*			
solicitar	*(to) apply for, request | applying for, requesting*			
sorprender	*(to) surprise | surprising*			
streaming (m)	*streaming*			
sueño (m)	*dream, sleep*			
sustituir	*(to) replace, substitute | replacing, substituting*			
suyo, suya, suyos, suyas	*his, hers (m, f, mpl, fpl) | yours (formal) (m, f, mpl, fpl) | theirs (m, f, mpl, fpl)*			
el suyo, la suya, los suyos, las suyas	*his, hers, its, yours (formal possessor), their (m, f, mpl, fpl)*			
tamaño (m)	*size, dimension*			
tema (m)	*topic, theme*			
tener ganas de	*(to) look forward to I looking forward to, (to) be keen to I being keen to*			
tener; tener que	*(to) have | having; (to) have to, must | having to*			
(a) ti	*(to) you (sing informal) (emph)*			
título (m)	*title, qualification*			
todo el mundo (m)	*everybody*			
trabajo (m)	*work, job, school assignment*			
traducir	*(to) translate | translating*			
traer	*(to) bring | bringing*			
tuyo, tuya, tuyos, tuyas	*yours (sing informal) (m, f, mpl, fpl)*			
el tuyo, la tuya, los tuyos, las tuyas	*yours (sing informal possessor) (m, f, mpl, fpl)*			
unión (f)	*union*			
universidad (f)	*university*			
universitario	*university*			
uso (m)	*use*			
verdad (f)	*truth*			
volar	*(to) fly | flying*			
vuelta (f)	*return*			
el vuestro, la vuestra, los vuestros, las vuestras	*yours (pl informal possessor) (m, f, mpl, fpl)*			

Foundation translation revision

Spanish to English

1 Read this Spanish paragraph and complete the partial translation below.

Me gusta chatear en línea. Uso mi móvil para mandar mensajes. Mi amiga juega al tenis el domingo. A veces vamos a un restaurante cerca de mi casa. Ayer fui al cine para ver una película de ciencia ficción.

I like to chat .... I use .... to send messages. My friend plays tennis .... Sometimes we go to a restaurant .... my house. Yesterday .... to the cinema .... a science fiction film.

2 Read the Spanish paragraph. Draw lines to match up the English sentence halves to complete the translation.

Mi familia es bastante guay. Me encanta pasar tiempo con mis abuelos. Mi hermano sigue a una cantante en la red. La semana pasada hice mucho ejercicio con un amigo. Creo que es muy importante tener buena salud.

1 My family
2 I love spending time
3 My brother follows
4 Last week I exercised
5 I think it's very important

a to have good health.
b a lot with a friend.
c is pretty cool.
d a singer on the net.
e with my grandparents.

3 Circle the correct word to complete the English translations.

1 Me encanta estudiar música y tecnología.

I love **learning** / **studying** music and **technology** / **history**.

2 Siempre saco buenas notas en los exámenes.

I **always** / **never** get good grades in **class** / **exams**.

3 En verano voy a un parque cerca del museo con mi clase.

In the **autumn** / **summer** I go to a park near the **square** / **museum** with my class.

5 En el pasado vivía en una ciudad mucho más tranquila.

In the past I **studied** / **lived** in a much **quieter** / **noisier** city.

4 Underline the two deliberate errors in each English translation.

1 Las redes sociales pueden ser peligrosas a veces, pero son también interesantes.

I think that social media can always be dangerous, but it is sometimes interesting.

2 La semana pasada me rompí la pierna y tuve que ir al hospital en coche con mi mamá.

Last week I broke my arm and had to go to the hospital by bus with my mum.

3 Sigo a una cantante famosa en línea porque hace mucho para ayudar a niños pobres.

I follow a famous actress online because she does a lot to protect poor children.

4 Cuando era más joven, me iba a la cama muy tarde y, al día siguiente, estaba demasiado cansado.

When I was younger, I used to go to bed very early and the next day, I was less tired.

5 Mi padre tendrá que aprender inglés porque tiene un nuevo trabajo en el extranjero.

My father will have to teach English because he has a new job in a school.

English to Spanish

1 Read these Spanish sentences and complete the partial translation below.

1 I go to school by bike.

Voy al ....

2 I want to protect the environment.

Quiero ....

3 My brother recycles bottles and newspapers.

Mi hermano ....

4 Last week, I took my own bag to the market.

La semana pasada ....

5 I think that the world is in danger.

Creo que el ....

2 Read the English paragraph. Number the boxes next to the Spanish sentences to put them in the correct order.

I am quite a responsible person and I always take my books to school. My best friend doesn't listen in class and always gets bad grades. Last week he was looking at his mobile phone when the professor saw it. Now he has to clean the playground every day for two weeks. He will have to work harder if he wants to pass the exams.

Él tendrá que trabajar más si quiere aprobar los exámenes. ☐

La semana pasada estaba mirando su teléfono móvil cuando el profesor lo vio. ☐

Soy una persona bastante responsable y siempre llevo mis libros al colegio. ☐

Mi mejor amigo no escucha en clase y siempre saca malas notas. ☐

Ahora tiene que limpiar el patio todos los días durante dos semanas. ☐

3 Look at the following text and highlight the English words with one colour and the Spanish words with another. Untangle the English and Spanish to create two texts that are translations of one another. Write them out on a separate sheet.

> No quiero to get married o tener children but espero to work en el extranjero. I'm looking forward to conocer a new people. El año pasado my older brother fue a Latin America. Creo que it's important aprender languages si you want to travel.

4 Translate these sentences into Spanish.

1 I play basketball on Saturdays. ....

2 Afterwards I have a sandwich in town. ....

3 I have good relationships with my family. ....

4 My sister is travelling in Spain at the moment. ....

5 Two years ago, I went on holiday with my cousins.

....

Higher translation revision

Spanish to English

1 Complete the English translations of these sentences.

1 Voy con unos amigos a un club para aprender sobre los ordenadores.

I go with ....

2 Ayer por la mañana mi hermano gemelo olvidó su contraseña.

Yesterday morning my ....

3 Esta noche tengo que colgar unas fotos de mi perro en mis redes sociales.

This evening ....

4 Mi padre puede conectarse a Internet para hablar con su pareja cuando está de viaje.

My father ....

2 Translate this paragraph into English on a separate sheet, using the phrases from the box.

we picked up	The good thing is that	and I can relax	with brown eyes
in the park	Last week	and we	I am tall and fair
he supports me a lot	with my best friend	with him	We have known each other
for ten years	I get along very well	never fight	rubbish together
near my house			

Soy alto y rubio con los ojos marrones. Me llevo muy bien con mi mejor amigo. La semana pasada recogimos la basura juntos en el parque cerca de mi casa. Lo bueno es que él me apoya mucho y puedo relajarme con él. Nos conocemos desde hace diez años y nunca nos peleamos.

3 Read the email and tick the three sentences correctly translated in English.

¿Sabías que el hijo de la vecina tiene su propia empresa de diseño en línea? Después de estudiar en la universidad, decidió trabajar por su cuenta. Ahora tiene otras personas trabajando con él y hacen proyectos con grandes compañías. ¡Mira su página web para ver lo bueno que es! Creo que ha tenido mucho éxito y ya es bastante rico. Sería mi sueño hacer algo así cuando sea mayor.

1 Did you know that the neighbour's son has his own online design company? ☐

2 Before studying at university, he decided to work for himself. ☐

3 Now he has another person working with him and they do projects with large shops. ☐

4 Check out their web page to see how good it is! ☐

5 I think he's had some success and he will soon be quite rich. ☐

6 It would be my dream to do something like that when I'm older. ☐

4 Translate this paragraph into English on a separate sheet.

Nunca he viajado a otros países. Quiero ir a un continente diferente porque se puede conocer diferentes culturas. Espero pasar un año en el extranjero después de terminar mi curso universitario. Cuando sea mayor, viviré allí con mi familia en América Latina. Mi hermano hizo un intercambio cultural en una ciudad donde tenemos numerosos familiares.

English to Spanish

1 Read this English paragraph and complete the partial translation below.

I have just returned from my grandmother's house. She lives in a small village in the countryside. Yesterday morning I did jobs in her garden to help her. The best thing about going there is that she cooks delicious food. We get on well because we like to talk and she tells me about the past.

.... de la casa .... Vive en
.... en el campo. Ayer .... tareas en su jardín
.... ir allí ....
cocina .... porque
.... conversar y .... del pasado.

2 Translate these verbs into Spanish and use them to complete the text below.

we used to go	....	I will enjoy	....
we had a good time	....	I have	....
we went	....	I met	....
we meet up	....	I would prefer	....
we returned	....	I will do	....

Normalmente, mis amigos y yo .... los sábados en la ciudad. En el pasado, ... al parque, pero hoy en día vamos al cine. Sin embargo, hace un mes .... a la costa para pasar unos días juntos. ...., pero llovió mucho, así que .... temprano a casa. Yo .... ir a la playa en verano. .... planes para ir al extranjero el año próximo para hacer un curso de idiomas. Lo .... en una ciudad grande y creo que .... mucho de esta experiencia. Hace dos años fui a otra región para practicar deportes y .... a mucha gente.

3 Look at the following text and highlight the English words with one colour and the Spanish words with another. Untangle the English and Spanish to create two texts that are translations of one another. Write them out on a separate sheet.

Tengo a job en una oficina. The work is aburrido and no me interesa. Last week I went with friends to manifestarnos against the gobierno. The lack of igualdad in the mundo laboral still me sorprende. I intend to luchar for the rights de los que work and defender women's rights.

4 Translate this paragraph into Spanish on a separate sheet.

In my house we try to save energy. I turn off the lights and the computer every night. My father always repairs and recycles articles when he can. Last week I bought some second-hand clothes in the market. I have decided to start a campaign to save water due to the problems of climate change.

Vocabulary learning strategies

There are many useful strategies for learning vocabulary. Try out different ones to find those that best suit your style of learning. Dedicate regular short bursts of active learning time to these methods.

Recording vocabulary

It is important to note down new vocabulary consistently as you come across it:

1. Write down new words in a list at the back of your exercise book.
2. Add new words to topic knowledge organisers or sentence builders.
3. Keep a separate notebook of vocabulary items (alphabetically or by topic).
4. Create mind maps of vocabulary for different topics or grammar points.
5. Use apps or online revision tools to create your own vocabulary lists.

Categorising vocabulary

1 Topic areas

- Organise your lists of words into topic areas, so they are easier to learn. Grammar points also make good 'topics', such as a focus on a particular tense. Create lists or make mind maps.
- Create a useful phrases list, or mind map, for words that are used across different topic areas. Include English translations for words you're not sure of yet.

2 Word families and groups

- When you come across a new word in a text, think about how it relates to other words you know. Group together words into their families.

  leer → *la lectura, leyendo*

- You can create rhyming families too: *artista, revista, turista, vista, entrevista, optimista.*

  Prefixes and suffixes are another way to group and learn words.

  Prefixes: for example *des-*: *desafortunadamente, descansar, desaparecer, desconocido.*

  Suffixes: for example *-idad*: *identidad, personalidad, posibilidad, felicidad, oportunidad.*

3 Synonyms and antonyms

- It's useful to learn words in pairs of synonyms (words that mean the same thing) and antonyms (words that mean the opposite).
- Create lists of synonyms and antonyms. You could organise these by grammar (nouns, adjectives, verbs, etc.) or by topic area, or as general lists to help learn words across topics.

Synonyms	Antonyms
mi barrio = mi zona	*la ciudad ≠ el campo*
el tiempo = el clima	*limpio ≠ sucio*
voy a pie = camino	*abierto ≠ cerrado*
hay que = se debe	*ganar ≠ perder*

Active learning strategies

1 Look-cover-write-check

- This strategy is good for learning and testing yourself on vocabulary.
  1. Look – study the word and say it aloud or in your head. Pay attention to the spelling.
  2. Cover – cover the word and say it again (aloud or in your head).
  3. Write – write down the word from memory, aiming for accurate spelling.
  4. Check – uncover the original word and mark your written version.
- If you make a mistake, add this word to another list to learn it and test yourself again.
- Covering the Spanish and writing the English is easier than covering the English and writing the Spanish. Aim to do both ways.

2 Revision cards

- Create your own mini flashcards using paper or card, or create them online.
- Cards can be made for single words, phrases or complete sentences. Write the Spanish on one side and the English translation on the other side.
- Use these cards to test yourself, or ask someone else to test you.

- Use sticky notes to display tricky words in places where you will read them often.

3 Games

Games are a fun and effective way to learn vocabulary. You can use games created by others (either from online sources or by your school), or you can create your own.

- Odd one out:

  pequeño grande caro barata limpio antiguo

  (The odd one out is *barata* as it cannot be used with a masculine noun.)
- Wordsearches and crosswords: create your own (online or by hand) with Spanish words then write out the English translations of the words to be found.
- Quizzes: create your own (online or on paper) to help revise vocabulary.
- Sentence snakes: write a sentence without any spaces and then ask someone to say or write the sentence correctly. Or ask someone to create some Spanish sentence snakes for you to decipher.

4 Active practice

Use these strategies to test how well you know the vocabulary you have been learning.

- **Be the teacher**

  Teach someone else how to pronounce these words in Spanish and what they mean.
- **Change the context**

  Use each word or phrase in a new sentence and write it down. Can you challenge yourself to use each word or phrase for a past topic you have learned?
- **Record yourself**

  Record yourself saying these words, on a phone or device, and then listen back to your recording. Can you improve on your pronunciation and record yourself again?
- **Keep categorising**

  Time yourself writing down your words in different ways. For example, can you write them in an alphabetical list, in size order or categorise them grammatically?

Alphabetical list	Size order list	Grammar focus list
la calle	*el transporte*	*el castillo*
el castillo	*la calle*	*el museo*
el museo	*la plaza*	*el transporte*
la plaza	*el museo*	*la calle*
el transporte	*el castillo*	*la plaza*

Translation strategies: Spanish to English

Here are some useful strategies to help you translate from Spanish into English. As you are doing translation exercises, refer back to these strategies to help you.

Reading for gist

When you are faced with the passage or sentence to translate from Spanish into English, it is really important to read it through to establish a general meaning, even if you know that there are some words you don't recognise or cannot immediately translate.

Word order

- Remember that word order can be different in Spanish and English. If there is an adjective in a sentence, for example, you will need to remember that most adjectives, including all colours, come after the word they describe in Spanish. So to translate *Llevo una chaqueta negra*, you would write 'I wear a black jacket', not 'a jacket black'.
- Be careful to remember subject pronouns when translating into English. Often you don't need to use them in Spanish because the verb form (usually the ending) makes it clear who is being referred to. So, if you had to translate *Van a Barcelona de vacaciones*, you would write, 'They go to Barcelona on holiday' because *van* is the third person plural form of the present tense of *ir*.
- Look out for object pronouns. These normally come in front of the verb in Spanish.

  Los profesores ***nos*** *ponen muchos deberes.* The teachers give **us** a lot of homework.

  Object pronouns can also be added to the end of infinitives in Spanish.

  *Mi hermano va a dar****me*** *un regalo.* My brother is going to give **me** a present.

  Be careful of *la*, *los* and *las* meaning 'her/to her' or 'them/to them' as they will come before the verb and must not be confused with the Spanish words for 'the' *(el/la/los/las)*.

  El chico ***la*** *quiere.* The boy loves **her**.

Using familiar language, context and common sense

Use familiar language, context and common sense to decode the meaning of unknown words.

- In the following sentence, identify the words you definitely know:

  Uso una aplicación para escuchar y bajar música de mis cantantes favoritos.

  You probably recognise *uso* (I use), *escuchar* (to listen), *música* (music) and *mis cantantes favoritos* (my favourite singers). *Una aplicación* is a cognate and looks very like the English word 'application' (app). Now you have 'I use an app to listen and … music of my favourite singers.' Ask yourself what makes sense in the context of the rest of the text. You then might guess the correct answer: *bajar* = to download.

- *Mi amigo está listo para salir.*

  It is important to read the whole text before you try to translate, to get an idea of the general meaning. This will help you to establish the context. *Listo* has two meanings in Spanish, 'clever' and 'ready', but here only one would work.

- *La gente ha dejado mucha basura en el parque; hay que limpiarlo.*

  You most likely know *gente* (people) and *parque* (park) and possibly *limpiar* (to clean); from that, you might be able to work out that *ha dejado* means 'has left' and, if the park needs cleaning, it is likely that *basura* means 'rubbish'.

Using cognates

- Look for cognates, words in both languages that have the same origin.
- Some look exactly the same in both languages: animal, festival, chocolate.
- Others look very similar: *bicicleta* (bicycle), *comenzar* (to commence), *difícil* (difficult).
- You can easily work out the meaning of these words in Spanish, even if you might not have known the word if you had been asked to translate it from Spanish into English.

False friends

Watch out for 'false friends': Spanish words that look similar to a word in English but actually have totally different meanings.

Mi hermana lava la ropa. *Me encanta la lectura.* *Tuve éxito en los exámenes.*

You might try the following translations:

My sister washes the rope. I love the lecture. I had an exit in the exams.

However, all three would be wrong! The correct translations are:

My sister washes the **clothes**. I love **reading**. **I was successful** in the exams.

Grammar

- Use **tense indicators** and your grammatical knowledge to help you translate the tense.

Present:	***Normalmente*** *vamos al cine los sábados.*	**Normally** we go to the cinema on Saturdays.
Preterite:	***Ayer*** *compré un móvil nuevo.*	**Yesterday** I bought a new mobile.
Future:	***El año próximo****, mi hermana irá a Madrid.*	**Next year** my sister will go to Madrid.

- Remember that you can translate some tenses in more than one way.

Present:	*La chica* ***lleva*** *un vestido verde.*	The girl **wears** a green dress. or The girl **is wearing** a green dress.
Imperfect:	***Estudiaba*** *ciencias.*	I **was studying** science. or I **used to study** science.

Translation skills

- Don't always try to translate word for word. You won't always find that one word in Spanish means one word in English.

  Suelo hacer ejercicio para mantenerme en forma.

  Suelo = I usually
  hacer ejercicio = exercise
  para mantenerme = to keep (myself)
  en forma = fit

- Don't be afraid to use different words or a different number of words to get a good translation, but don't stray too far from the meaning or make random guesses. It is, however, important to account for every word in a translation, even if some words don't need translating or if you need to add words for the sentence to make sense.

  Jugaba ***al*** *fútbol los fines de semana.* He used to play football **at** the weekend.

  In this example, *al* does not need translating from the Spanish *al fútbol*, but we have to add 'at' in English before 'the weekend'.

- Read your translation to yourself to check that it makes sense and sounds natural.

  Odio también llevar uniforme.

  You could translate this example as 'I also hate wearing uniform' or 'I hate wearing uniform too', but not as 'I hate also wearing uniform', as this sounds clumsy in English. Play around with the word order until your English translation sounds natural.

Translation strategies: English to Spanish

Here are some different strategies for when you are translating from English into Spanish. When you have a passage or sentence to translate into Spanish, read the whole thing through once. Then work sentence by sentence or phrase by phrase, bearing the following strategies in mind.

Grammar – verbs

- Think carefully about the **verb forms** you need. Who is the subject of the verb (who is doing the action)? Is it more than one person? Make sure you know your verb endings.

  We went to Spain. ***Fuimos*** *a España.*

  He went to Spain. ***Fue*** *a España.*

- Always read the English carefully to make sure you have identified which tense needs to be used in Spanish. Look for clues such as **time markers** to help you.

  Last week I visited my friend. ⟶ preterite tense needed

  Next week, she will play tennis. ⟶ future tense needed

  But remember that to say how long you have been doing/have done something for in Spanish, you use ***desde hace*** + **the present tense**, when you would use the **perfect tense** in English.

  We have played tennis **for** six years. ***Jugamos*** *al tenis* ***desde hace*** *seis años.*

- Take care with **reflexive verbs** in Spanish as these aren't always obvious from the English. Reflexive verbs are frequent in daily routine translations at GCSE.

  I get up at 7.00. ***Me*** *levanto a las siete.*

- Remember that Spanish uses infinitives for activities where English uses words ending in '-ing'.

  I like going to the cinema. *Me gusta ir al cine.*

- You might have to use **modal verbs**, so look out for 'can', 'must', 'should', 'allowed to' and remember that these verbs are followed by the infinitive in Spanish.

  You **should** eat fruit every day. ***Se debería*** *comer fruta todos los días.*

When translating verb forms into Spanish, you won't normally need to translate the subject pronouns (I, you, he, she) as the verb ending will tell the reader who is doing the action. It may be necessary in the third person, to distinguish between 'he', 'she', 'it' or the formal 'you' (*usted*).

Grammar – nouns and adjectives

Gender, articles and adjectival agreement and position are also very important when you are translating nouns into Spanish. Remember that the ***-o*** ending changes to ***-a*** when the adjective describes a feminine noun, and to ***-os*** or ***-as*** when the noun is plural. If the adjective ends in a consonant, it does not change in the feminine singular, but you need to add **-es** in the plural, for either gender.

Grammar – time phrases

Learn common time and frequency phrases: yesterday (*ayer*), today (*hoy*), tomorrow (*mañana*), every day (*todos los días*). 'In the morning' is translated as *por la mañana*, 'in the afternoon' as *por la tarde* and 'in the evening' as *por la noche*.

Grammar – useful little words

Build up your vocabulary with words such as intensifiers (*bastante, muy*), quantifiers (*mucho/a(s), un poco de*), conjunctions (*pero, porque*) and prepositions (*con, desde*).

Word order

You need to think carefully about word order when you are translating into Spanish. Remember the rules for adjectives and object pronouns.

- Most **adjectives**, including all colours, come after the noun they describe.

  Spain has lots of **historical** monuments. *España tiene muchos monumentos* ***históricos***.
- **Object pronouns** come before the verb.

  She has given **me** a present. ***Me*** *ha dado un regalo.*
- Remember, when translating verbs such as 'like' and 'love' in English, you need to think carefully about how you construct the sentence. For example, 'I like football' would be translated as *Me gusta el fútbol* which literally translates as 'Football is pleasing to me'.

Translation skills

- Be careful with words that we miss out in English but that must be there in Spanish, and vice versa. This often happens with **articles**.

  I don't like coffee. *No me gusta* ***el*** *café.*

  On Sundays he plays football. *Los domingos juega* ***al*** *fútbol.*

  My brother wants to be **a** teacher. *Mi hermano quiere ser profesor.*
- Avoid translating word for word when you translate into Spanish. Be particularly careful with the **present continuous** in English, which sometimes does not need to be directly translated into Spanish. Use the present continuous tense only for something that you are doing right now.

  I **am listening** to music. ***Estoy escuchando*** *música.*

  I **am studying** maths at university. ***Estudio*** *matemáticas en la universidad.*

  Similarly, the **imperfect tense** in Spanish is a single word.

  I **used to play** / I **was playing** tennis. ***Jugaba*** *al tenis.*

  The same is true for 'will' in the **future tense**. It is not a separate word in Spanish.

  I **will go** to Spain in winter. ***Iré*** *a España en invierno.*
- In English, we would sometimes say 'The city I visited' instead of the fuller 'The city that I visited'. In Spanish, *que* is needed.

  La ciudad ***que*** *visité.*
- When you are asked to translate from English into Spanish, you might need to look carefully at the sentence or part of the sentence that comes before the one you are translating.

  Last year we bought a house in Spain. It's not very comfortable and it's too small.

  In this example, it is important to know to what 'it' in the second sentence refers. The noun is *casa* and, because it is a feminine noun, the endings of the adjectives need to agree. The correct translation will be:

  El año pasado compramos una casa en España. No es muy cómoda y es demasiado pequeña.
- If you don't know how to say something in Spanish, don't panic! Try to think of a **synonym**, a similar word, or another way to say it using the vocabulary that you do know.
- Check your spelling, accents and grammar.
- If you have time, it is a good idea to try to translate what you have written back into English, to see if it really does match the translation you were asked to do.

Notes